CARD WEAVING

Ruth J. Katz

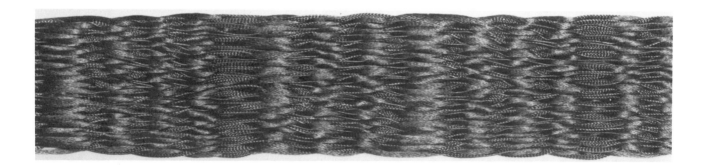

VNR VAN NOSTRAND REINHOLD COMPANY
New York Cincinnati Toronto London Melbourne

**With appreciation to
Y. King,
My faithful friend**

All photographs by Malcolm Varon, New York, unless otherwise credited. Drawings by the author.

Printed in the United States of America.
Designed by Loudan Enterprises

Published in 1977 by Van Nostrand Reinhold Company
A division of Litton Educational Publishing, Inc.
450 West 33rd Street, New York, NY 10001, U.S.A.

Van Nostrand Reinhold Limited
1410 Birchmount Road, Scarborough, Ontario M1P 2E7, Canada

Van Nostrand Reinhold Australia Pty. Limited
17 Queen Street, Mitcham, Victoria 3132, Australia

Van Nostrand Reinhold Company Limited
Molly Millars Lane, Wokingham, Berkshire, England

16 15 14 13 12 11 10 9 8 7 6 5 4 3 2 1

Library of Congress Cataloging in Publication Data

Katz, Ruth J.
  Card Weaving

  Bibliography: p.
  Includes index.
  1. Card weaving. I. Title.
TT848.K33   746.1′4   73-16712
ISBN 0-442-24261-1

ACKNOWLEDGMENTS

I wish to acknowledge the kindness and prompt cooperation of the many researchers and curators in the museums I queried and visited, who found the time to supply me with photographs and information.

I would like to thank my editors Leslie Wenger and Nancy Newman Green, for their valuable guidance, suggestions, and endless patience; my family, for their understanding and encouragement; all my friends for their support and willingness to share my trials and tribulations. A special thanks to Julie Schwartz for her active interest and efforts and to Donna Sinanian for her inspiration. My deepest gratitude to my dear friend and colleague, Malcolm Varon, for his unfailing generosity and professional expertise.

Decorative bands used as chapter openers are:

p 3. A Swedish ribbon used as an apron tie. (Collection Hamburgisches Museum für Völkerkunde, Hamburg, Germany)

p 4. Close-up detail of Figure 7-3. (Victoria and Albert Museum, London, England, Crown Copyright)

pp 8, 17. Bands from the 20th century, woven by the Danish weaver Lis Ahlmann. (Danish Museum of Decorative Art, Copenhagen)

pp 24, 44, 74. Modern card-woven bands from Denmark. (Danish Museum of Decorative Art, Copenhagen)

pp 90, 101, 110, 145. Watch bands of silk by the Danish weaver Elizabeth Budde-Lund, made in 1947; exhibited by the Danish Handicraft Guild, 1947. (Danish Museum of Decorative Art, Copenhagen)

p 147. A Persian band a little over one inch wide woven with gold, silver, and pink borders and black-and-white double-faced weave bearing the inscription. (Museum of History, Berne, Ethnographic Department)

p 149. An example of Persian double-faced weave with an Arabic inscription in red and white. The borders are blue, green, and yellow. This is a very long piece, over nine feet long. (Museum of History, Berne, Ethnographic Department)

Contents

1. Introduction

Card weaving (also known as tablet weaving) is one of the oldest forms of weaving known today. Perhaps it is because of its age that it is a somewhat primitive and time-consuming craft. It is, however, a unique method and an easy process to master. Card weaving enables the weaver to produce narrow bands of multi-ply (usually four-ply, but sometimes three-, six-, seven-, or even eight-ply) fabric of extraordinary strength and durability. Today's weaver, because of clever inventions unknown to the ancients, can weave fabric bands as wide as a foot or more.

The actual weaving is executed with the aid of small tablets or cards, hence its name. The finished pieces are unique because of both their means of construction and resultant flexibility. They alone can be used for purposes for which no other woven fabric would be suitable. This combination of pliability and durability which characterizes card weaving makes it a singular form of weaving; because of this, there are needs for card weaving which, essentially, cannot be met by other hand-woven bands.

Card-woven bands are ideal for: sandal straps, backpack supports, bag handles, valise grips, guitar bands, venetian blind pulls, apron strings, dog leashes, wrist-watch bands, belts, shoelaces (particularly for ice skates and sports shoes), etc.

In addition to these uses where strength is a primary concern, card-woven bands, because of the wealth of designs produced in them, are also perfect for trim and ornamentation: hat bands, garment trim of all types (particularly on items woven by other means), drapery trim, hair ornaments, headbands, neck pieces, bookmarks, neckties, sashes, pot holders, place mats, wall decorations, hangings, etc.

1-1. A linen watch strap woven on twelve cards.

4

It is obvious that card weaving has many applications; its uses are limitless, and the more imaginative the weaver, the more valuable card weaving will be to him.

As pointed out earlier, it is a very slow process because it is largely a nonmechanical one. It requires time, patience, and care to thread the cards, and is, therefore, not used commercially. Once the cards are threaded, however, weaving progress is very rapid.

All aspects of the setting-up process are important. There is no actual loom for card weaving, but rather the cards themselves are used to *create* the loom. That is to say, until recently, you could not go into a store and purchase a card-weaving loom. You could purchase cards and the necessary accoutrements, but not a special loom. Recently, however, several looms became available on the market to help the card weaver.

Unfortunately, using a loom can be somewhat restrictive, in that it tends to limit the length of the working warp and may even slow progress by decreasing control of the warp tension. The looms illustrated in Figures 1-3 through 1-6, however, can all be used for card weaving. An inkle-type loom is also shown, as this can be adapted for card weaving by removing the heddles and substituting the cards.

I prefer, however, to construct a loom such as the one shown in Figure 4-19. The weaver who opts to do this must be ingenious and resourceful. Many methods are possible, and while seeking out one which suits you, do not be surprised to find some looms functional machinations, and others back-breaking Rube Goldberg-styled contraptions. It takes a little experimentation, but you will find the right loom for your personal use.

I have a method that is both comfortable and portable. Experimenting to discover the best loom for yourself is well worth the effort.

Card weaving gives the novice an opportunity to learn to weave readily and enjoy the delight of seeing some four-hundred yards of fiber become a handsome belt in three hours! Once the technique of warping is mastered, the garment practically weaves itself. The advanced weaver will probably enjoy studying the subtle nuances of design variations achieved by minor changes in threading, as well as the more startling pattern differences which result when advanced techniques are applied. There are, indeed, limitless, sophisticated corollaries to the basic card-weaving principle, and advanced students will find an infinite range of elaborate patterns literally at their fingertips. After a short time the card weaver will be able to draft his own patterns. Any craftsperson familiar with handweaving will find that the combination of card-woven and traditionally woven items results in singularly beautiful completed works. The rich design of card-woven trim complements the loom-woven piece and generally adds a finished look to a garment.

On the other hand, not all card weaving is so sophisticated. Basic card weaving is so easy that even children can do it and produce satisfying pieces in no time at all. Indeed, because of its utter simplicity, card weaving is a part of many school craft programs and is integrated into physical therapy programs both at home and abroad.

For the student who knows nothing of weaving it may be difficult to understand at first just how card weaving differs from other kinds of weaving. It would be an error to say that card weaving is not loom weaving, for as mentioned above, the cards *do* create a loom. The main difference between a card-woven item and, for example, a piece of material, a tapestry, or a wall hanging (all three being familiar loom projects) is that card weaving renders the finished product warp-faced.

What does this mean? Simply put, this is a way of saying that the warp makes the design and not the

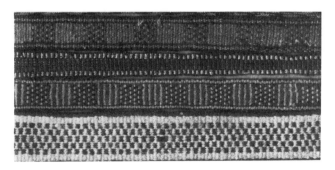

1-2. Shoelaces from Sweden woven in a variety of simple patterns. (Collection Hamburgisches Museum für Völkerkunde, Hamburg, Germany)

filling (or weft, as it is also known). Both the concept and implementation of card weaving are exactly opposite those of tapestry weaving. In a tapestry, the fiber for the warp is all generally of the same strength, texture, and color and serves *not* as a decoration, but rather as a foundation. In a finished tapestry, the warp does not usually show; it is not a part of the design, but rather is a functional structure on which to place (or weave) the design. The scene, inscription, or pattern of the tapestry is made by the filling. The weaver controls the design by determining over or under which warp ends the filling travels. The result is a tapestry with little or no trace of the warp, but rather a design *supported by* the warp.

Fabric is woven in much the same way, but the warp shows and is an integral and vital part of the design. The fabric is, therefore, created by the interlocking of the warp and the filling. Limitless combinations of different colors and varied textures of fibers, as well as endless threading patterns, are all responsible for creating the myriad of fabrics produced by the textile industry today. A creative weaver can vary warp, filling, and threading ad infinitum and never create the same fabric twice.

Card weaving is executed in a different manner, and, therefore, the results are not the same. The warp is the more important consideration and is likewise the more dynamic partner of the two; by

1-3. Two looms for card weaving—a large frame-style loom at which the weaver is working allows for greater width, and a backstrap-style loom for narrower bands, in foreground. (Some Place, Berkeley, California)

extension, then, the variations of the warp in both color and texture are also noteworthy. The design is a direct result of the way in which the warp ends are arranged (or threaded), as well as how they are passed over and under the filling. Almost always the filling remains constant and is of little conse-

quence in the overall design, as it never significantly shows on the face of the weaving. Generally, it shows only at the edges and once in a while on the surface of the weaving (when the direction of the cards is changed, which is discussed later). The weaver can change the fiber used as filling, but no appreciable variation will occur as a result of it.

Assembling the warp ends is obviously of the utmost importance and is the key to developing new designs. Directing the position of the warp ends could be a very painstaking task, were it not for the tablets or cards on which they are assembled. The warp ends are threaded through the cards, which then act as guides for them. In this manner, the cards correspond pretty much to the heddles on the conventional-style loom through which the warp is similarly "threaded." The warp ends stay channelled properly and tangle-free because of the cards. Both ends of the warp are then secured to stationary objects; more often than not, one of the stationary objects is the weaver himself!

In this fashion the "loom" is created. The weaver exercises control over the cards by turning them. As the cards are turned, new "openings" are created, through which the filling will pass. The opening is called a shed, and as it opens and closes with the turning of the cards, the filling thread locks each turn into place. Chapter 3 deals with the equipment of card weaving and elucidates these points.

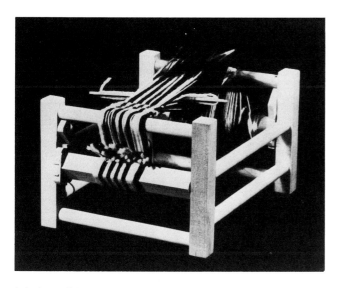

1-4. A small loom converted to accommodate card weaving. (The Handcrafters, Waupun, Wisconsin)

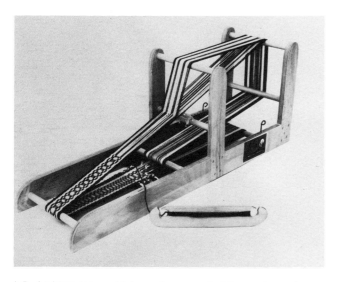

1-5. An inkle loom which can be converted for card weaving. The shuttle is ideal for band weaving. (Lily Mills, Shelby, North Carolina)

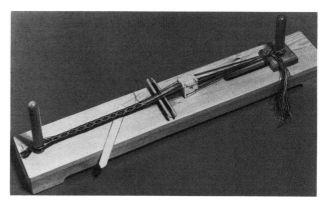

1-6. A very simple loom; one peg is adjustable to vary the tension. A loom similar to this can be constructed with nails and a board. (Dryad, Leicester, England)

2. History

Card weaving is one of the oldest forms of weaving. It has not, however, been practiced continuously throughout the ages: it was a lost art for several hundred years. It is through the persistent research of Margarethe Lehmann-Filhés of Berlin in the late nineteenth century that we know as much as we do today about card weaving. She unearthed cards in a museum in Denmark, and with a duplicate set she began to investigate the art. Her findings, published in a definitive account, generated much enthusiasm among both craftspeople and anthropologists. Their combined inquiries and subsequent documentation are responsible for our present knowledge of the art.

Some scholars date card weaving as far back as 4000 B.C., claiming the contents of an excavated tomb as evidence. The contents of the grave included the skeleton of a woman whose fragmented dress is sashed with what appears to be a card-woven belt. Other researchers maintain that no fabrics bearing design were actually woven until 1500 B.C. It is, however, generally believed that the Egyptians *knew of* card weaving and many designs on garments found both on statues and in drawings could have been produced by card weaving (Figure 2-1).

Similarly, the thin linen strips with which the Egyptians mummified their dead could have been

2-1. Typical Egyptian designs such as this one are common on statuary and drawings from the period.

produced by card weaving as well.* The famous Girdle of Rameses III, used for burial purposes, is the most celebrated and debated of Egyptologists' finds. It dates from 1200 B.C. and has intricate patterns as well as an elaborate overall design distinguishing it from many ordinary girdles. It is over seventeen feet long and varies in width from five to less than two inches. Over 1,600 linen warp ends—red, yellow, green, blue, and natural—compose the design. The Girdle itself is in excellent condition and can be viewed today at the Liverpool Museum. (See Figure 2-2 and Color Plate C-1)

It has been alternately proved and refuted that this colorful band was produced by card weaving. Academicians, as well as weavers, have debated this topic for many years and it was the subject of no less than three articles between 1912 and 1923 in the scholarly *Annals of Archaeology and Anthropology*. It was also the topic of a highly informative French treatise by two researchers named Van Gennep and Jéquier. Their 1916 book, *Le Tissage aux Cartons et son Utilisation Décorative dans l'Egypte Ancienne*, asserts that the Girdle of Rameses was, in fact, card woven. Van Gennep felt certain that card weaving was an invention of the Egyptians and that it reached its full development sometime between 3000–2400 B.C. The two researchers actually included in their book handwoven reproductions of Egyptian specimens. The book is extraordinary and the beautifully handwoven samples are well worth viewing.

Two more researchers, Roth and Crowfoot, offer support to their theory that the Girdle is *not*, in fact, card woven. They cite many technical points regarding the texture and structure of the Girdle, and underscore the fact that no other fabrics or cards have appeared to support Van Gennep's and Jéquier's theories. They stress that illustrations on

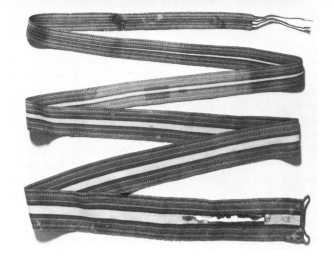

2-2. The Girdle of Rameses III in its entirety. (City of Liverpool Museum, England)

monuments and statues, as well as drawings, could easily be effigies of non-nationals from countries where card weaving was practiced. They further emphasize that no tablets or card-weaving implements that date from pre-Coptic times have been found in Egypt. The earliest known tablets are from the tomb of the mummy "Euphemia, La Brodeuse" (The Embroider); these tablets are not nearly so old as the Girdle. Their conclusion is that the famous Girdle is woven on some other form of primitive braid-type loom.

In 1930, a German weaver, Frau Staudigel-Scharlau duplicated the Girdle using both four- and six-holed cards for the Museum für Völkerkunde in Leipzig. Many weavers felt her copy was fairly accurate and proved the Girdle was card woven.

In Volume IX of the *Liverpool Bulletin*, in a highly technical and detailed article, Herr Otfried Staudigel reaffirms this theory, and states that the lack of evidence of card-weaving equipment is not conclusive proof that card weaving was unknown to the Egyptians. He adds that the cards found in the tomb of Euphemia are in a state of disintegration and implements dating from pre-Coptic times may simply be lost forever.

In a subsequent article in Volume X of that same publication, Elizabeth Crowfoot rejects the theory behind the 1930 Leipzig replica: The copy is not precise and even if card weaving *can* render an exact duplication of the Girdle, it does not prove that the belt was, in fact, woven with cards.

---

*Most civilizations buried their dead in complete regalia—from basic garments to accessories to miscellaneous trappings, as in the case of Queen Asa (mentioned on page 10), who was buried with a loom as well. The Egyptians, however, generally mummified their dead and it is for that and other reasons that we have not found rich examples of their clothing in excavated tombs. (The Girdle of Rameses III is a rare exception.) There have been some discoveries made of linen burial strips on bodies excavated at Qua el Kebir which date from the Coptic Period, and these narrow bands could easily have been card woven.

And so, the discussion goes on. . . . Having seen the famous Girdle in photographs only, I do not wish to offer an opinion, but can say without fear of reprisal that card weaving is, indeed, one of the oldest forms of weaving known today.

It may date back to the twenty-second dynasty in Egypt (945 B.C.), from which period several woven linen strips were discovered. With certainty, however, it dates back to Coptic times, as evidenced by the findings of the Gayet Excavations in upper Egypt, which took place during 1905–7. In these expeditions the most well-known pieces were unearthed at Antinoe—that is the twenty-five four-holed cards found with the Mummy Euphemia (already mentioned)—known as the "Sycamore Tablets." There were, however, other cards found, all believed to be from the Early Coptic Period. (See Figures 2-3 and 2-4)

In Norway, card weaving dates back to at least A.D. 850, as evidenced by the Oseberg Burial, (see Figure 2-5) unearthed in 1904. In the grave were two looms, one completely intact, with fifty-two cards and part of a woven band. The other loom was fragmented, but enough of the cards were preserved to determine that they were made of beech. This was the tomb of Queen Asa, a woman of aristocratic society, and her servant, both of whom had been provided with looms for the next life.

In Denmark, card weaving may date as far back as the Bronze Age (1500–900 B.C.). There were several bands found which support this theory—but their construction is so simple that they suggest simple finger weaving. Two-holed cards (which produce a plain weave such as these bands have) have been f und in a Stone Age dwelling in Als. Whether card weaving was known at this time, then, is debatable; it is, however, likely that it was practiced in the Celtic Iron Age, as evidenced by the discovery in Western Jutland (in the Dejbjerg Bog) of two cards, dating from 100 B.C.

On the Continent, it may date back to the time of Pliny the Elder who wrote in his *Naturalis Historia* that Alexandrian weavers used heddles and Gallic weavers used "little shields."

2-3. Six wooden tablets, from the Coptic Period, excavated around Antinoe during 1905–7 by Gayet. (Louvre, Paris, Department of Coptic Antiquities)

2-4. Three wooden tablets with etched designs, excavated about 1890, from Planig, Germany. (Städtische Kulturinstitute Worms, Germany)

2-5. Threaded loom, dating from A.D. 850. (Collection of Antiquities, Oslo University, Norway)

With such incomplete and scattered data, it is hard to say whether card weaving has its origins in the Middle East or in Scandinavia. Most of the finds we have today are from Scandinavia, North Africa, and Asia. (See Figures 2-6 through 2-8 and Color Plate C-2.)

It continued to be practiced throughout the Middle Ages and one sees its applications throughout the world. In the Orient, silks were woven on six-holed cards to create a finely detailed, luxurious, and gleaming overall effect. In Burma, the Himalayas, and India the greatest need for card weavings came from the Church, where elegant weavings were used as ties for religious books and monks' garments and often had religious inscriptions woven into them. Card-woven bands were used outside the Church for women's shawl and veil trims. Indeed, card-woven fringes were added to sixteenth- and seventeenth-century quilts made in Bengal under the patronage of Europeans. (Such a quilt was on display in 1970 at the Victoria and Albert Museum in London on loan from the Swedish Royal Collections.) In the Middle East, detailed metal work was combined with card weaving to create rich and sophisticated objects. In Persia, the artisans' works were particularly skillful and often sold as export items. In Armenia, Bulgaria, Greece, and Turkey, card weaving was used to produce colorful and functional belts and garters. In England, France, and Spain, it was used mostly in the Church and on tapestries. In Germany, silk bands were used as book bindings.

It is likely that as commerce (and strife—i.e., the sweeping raids of the Mongol hordes) increased between East and West, the intermingling of their disparate fabrics became popular. By the ninth century, card weavings became more abundant in the Church and less confined to woolen fibers. Many examples of the delicate and detailed silk bands woven for religious purposes can be seen today in museums throughout Europe. Card-woven bands became an elegant trim for the garments of secular princes, as well as of Church officials. Two of the best known examples of this period (mid-ninth–early tenth centuries) are the maniples of the Bishop Witgarius of Augsburg (Germany) and St. Cuthbert of Durham (England).

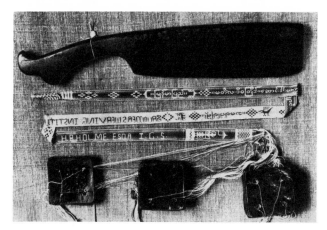

2-6. A weaving loom from Burma, including large beater, set of tanned, polished, and lacquered tablets, and partially woven band with an inscription. (Dryad, Leicester, England)

2-7. A loom for card weaving from Hara S'rira, Djerba Island (Tunisia), probably dating from the early 20th century. The warp ends are put through a reed, or comblike device to keep them tangle-free. (Collection Hamburgisches Museum für Völkerkunde, Hamburg, Germany)

2-8. A loom for card weaving from Iceland (Collection Hamburgisches Museum für Völkerkunde, Hamburg, Germany)

As silks became more widely used, the finished pieces took on a richer, less "folksy" finish. Eventually, gold threads were added to complement the silks and create a lustrous band. It is likely that ultimately this growing practice of adding metallic fibers gave way to the brocading of details and embroidering of inscriptions. As these dazzling techniques increased, the popularity of plainly woven tablet bands decreased. Silk tablet bands most likely were used with these embellishments as the latter type of work became more stylish.

Card weaving could not be duplicated for functional purposes (animal bridles and saddlery, for example), but for decorative purposes (such as book and chest bindings), it could be replaced by brocades and embroideries, which certainly were not as strong, but were well received for their elaborate design qualities.

Slowly this ancient art disappeared and did not reappear until the late nineteenth century. Then, sporadically, it resurfaced in such places as India, Sweden, Bukhara, Denmark, and Germany. A sprinkling of unconnected data aroused the curiosity of the scholar Margarethe Lehmann-Filhés and others. Such enthusiasm was generated in Germany that in 1902 *der Bazar Illustrierte damen Zeitung* (fashion magazine, counterpart of today's *Harper's Bazaar*) printed a lengthy article about card weaving, including instructions and patterns. In the United States *Bazaar's* fashion pages depicted frocks with braided or woven trim, and all were accorded proper mention.

Today, there are many articles on card weaving in anthropological and ethnographic journals. In an article published in 1970, it was noted that card weaving was practiced in the early part of this century in such diverse places as Celebes, West Java, and Morocco. In 1973, at the 13th International Congress of Anthropological and Ethnological Sciences, a paper was presented which dealt exclusively with card weaving in Yemen, where it was a very special art, reserved for several Jewish families alone, passed from generation to generation.

It is lucky for us that this card-weaving renaissance occurred, although the first book (in English) on the topic did not appear until about 1920. Thanks to diligent scholarly research we have a wealth of information on this subject. If it had not been for Margarethe Lehmann-Filhés' determination, we would be in much the same position *she* was when faced with the existence of the tablets, but unaware of how to *use* them!

2-9. A German band from the 12–13th century with the inscription "(n) Omine Domine No(stri)." The silver buckle is enameled and dates from the 14th century. (Diocesan Museum of Augsburg, Germany)

2-10. An ecclesiastical band from Upper Germany, dating from the 9–10th century. The band is woven in red silk; this section of the inscription reads "Nomine." (Diocesan Museum of Augsburg, Germany)

2-11. A 12th-century Islamic band, embellished with gold brocading. Notice the fragmented borders with geometric squares and diagonal lines. (Victoria and Albert Museum, London, England, Crown Copyright)

2-12. Black-and-green headband from Morocco with ties at the ends for fastening. The central design of squares over rectangles is reminiscent of the Mogen David, or Jewish Star—a typical design woven by Jewish weavers from Yemen for their Islamic patrons. (Museum für Völkerkunde und Schweizerisches Museum für Volkskunde, Basel, Switzerland)

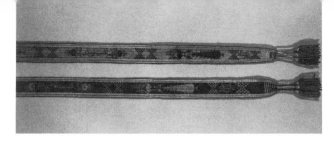

2-13. A 19th-century band from Burma, with typical, recurring tree-of-life-with-peacock motif. The inscription is in Pali. (Courtesy of the Cooper-Hewitt Museum of Decorative Arts and Design, Smithsonian Institution)

2-15. An exceptional example of card weaving from Gondar, Abyssinia. This 17–18th-century curtain tapestry is made from heavy silk in three widths. The diamonds/lozenges/diagonals in the left-hand panel are typical of Egyptian patterns. (Royal Ontario Museum, Toronto, Canada)

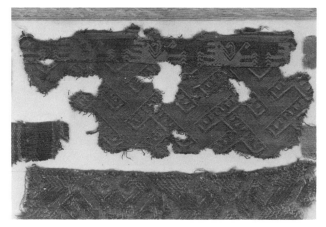

2-14. An elegant, 14th-century French weaving used in the Church. The body of the band is silk, embellished with brocade and gold and silver embroidery. (Victoria and Albert Museum, London, England, Crown Copyright)

2-16. Fragments of a card-woven band from Fort Miram, East Turkestan, dating from about A.D. 800. This is part of the discoveries made by Sir Aurel Stein in an expedition in 1906–8. (Trustees of the British Museum, London, England)

13

2-19. A Sicilian stole for religious purposes made with a silk warp and gold brocading, dating from the 12–13th centuries. (Victoria and Albert Museum, London, England, Crown Copyright)

2-20. A celebrated example of card weaving, used as a strap for a gun-powder flask. The designs are typical—tree of life with a peacock alternating with vases of flowers. The band is silk and the inscription reads "Blessed Be, Happy Be, Mighty Be." (Museum of History, Berne, Ethnographical Department)

2-17. A silk, linen, and metallic ecclesiastical stole from Cologne, Germany, probably dating from the 16th century. (Courtesy of the Cooper-Hewitt Museum of Decorative Arts and Design, Smithsonian Institution)

2-18. Two fragments of an old Egyptian band with red squares in a pattern typical of the period. Notice the technique of braiding the warp ends to finish the edges. (Museum für Völkerkunde und Schweizerisches Museum für Völkskunde, Basel, Switzerland)

2-21. A typical Persian card-woven band, probably used as a religious book tie. The tree-of-life pattern is seen here without the usual peacock while the vase of flowers is replaced by a very long-stemmed tuliplike bud. (Museum of History, Berne, Ethnographical Department)

2-23. Two very simple Indian bands. (Ethnological Museum, St. Gall, Collection Volkart)

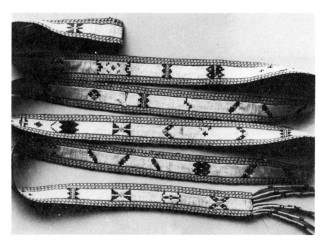

2-24. An extraordinary Bulgarian belt with wrapped warp ends, embroidery, and a crude type of brocading. (Collection Hamburgisches Museum für Völkerkunde, Hamburg, Germany)

2-25. One example of card weaving from China. This piece is from Shanghai and measures four and one-half feet long. (Ethnological Museum, St. Gall, Collection Volkart)

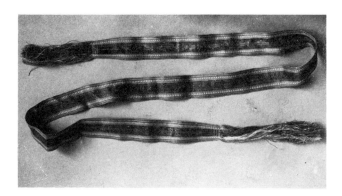

2-22. A finely woven Persian example with very elaborate floral motifs. (Ethnological Museum, St. Gall, Collection Volkart)

2-26. An inscribed band from Burma. (Ethnological Museum, St. Gall, Collection Volkart)

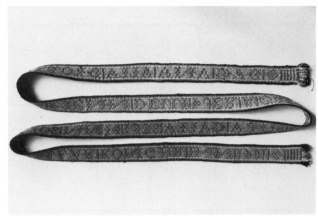

2-27. An inscribed band from Iceland. (Ethnological Museum, St. Gall, Collection Volkart)

2-28. This woolen, fringed camel girdle is from the Nubian Desert. (Museum für Völkerkunde und Schweizerisches Museum für Völkskunde, Basel, Switzerland)

2-29. Detail from the tapestry series "L'Histoire de la Vierge," depicting the life of the Virgin. The tapestry dates from 1530 and shows a loom with six-holed tablets and a partially woven band. (Tapestry from the Musée des Beaux Arts, Reims; photo courtesy of the Ministère des Affaires Culturelles, Paris, France)

3. Equipment

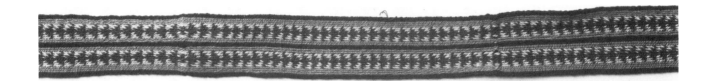

Materials are listed below with brief descriptions; specific directions for their use are presented later in greater detail. Most of these items will be readily found in the home. The cards and a beater/shuttle are the only pieces of true weaving equipment, but you can make your own cards, and there are common household substitutes for the beater/shuttle. Suppliers of card weaving materials are provided at the end of this book.

3-1. Supplies for card weaving include cards, shuttle/beater, a hanger, measuring tape (and/or ruler), tape, scissors, paper and pencil, and assorted cords.

CARDS

Naturally, the essential equipment required is a set of cards! These weaving cards are readily available from many weaving shops both in the United States and abroad. For the most part, cards are very inexpensive, considering one set will probably last a lifetime. It is not unreasonable then, to pay three or four dollars for a set of one hundred cards. You can make your own cards, but the process is time-consuming and the results often not satisfying.

The ambitious reader, however, may wish to try his hand at it. To construct cards, use a firm material, such as cardboard, Bristol board, or oak-tag. (An ideal material is "170-lb. index" used by printers.) Plastic or celluloid—Lucite and plexiglass—is fine, if the proper implements are available for cutting. The cutting is very important: The finished edges of the cards should be clean and clear of all debris. Fuzzy edges will prevent the cards from sliding through the warp ends, and ultimately the cards will stick. Similarly, sharp edges will catch, fray, and cut the warp ends.

Cut the cards into three-and-one-half-inch squares. They can be larger or smaller (see Figure 3-2), but cards of about that size seem to work best. The corners must be rounded to ease the weaving process. Punch a hole, roughly one-quarter inch to three-quarters inch in from the edge of each outer corner. The holes punched should be round and about one-quarter inch to three-eighths inch in diameter. The circumference of the hole must also be very smooth. It is particularly important that the holes be free of loose cuttings because as the cards are turned, the holes rub constantly against the warp ends. The further away the hole is punched from the corner, the closer the warp ends will be to each other (since they pass through these holes) and the smaller the shed will be. If the holes are put nearer the corners, then the shed will be wider (see Figure 3-4).

Most patterns call for anywhere from ten to fifty cards. Perhaps it is clear now why most weavers prefer to buy cards rather than make them. Considering that the construction of the cards is so delicate a procedure, it is amazing that ancient weavers were able to use the materials they did. Cards were commonly made of soft bone; thin, polished wood (usually beech and sycamore); tanned leather (camel, deer), often polished and lacquered; tortoise shell; paper of all sorts, including parchments, cardboards, and even playing cards with holes burned in them; and sheet bronze.

Advanced weavers may wish to experiment with triangular, pentagonal, hexagonal, and even octagonal cards, with three, five, six, and eight holes respectively. The basic principles involved when weaving with cards of these shapes are the same as with square, four-holed cards. The designs will be different because the pattern repeats will occur at different intervals. Turning these cards requires great care and much practice. The sheds are not always as clearly defined, either, as with four-holed cards.

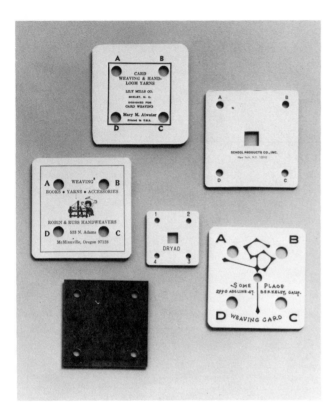

3-2. These are but a few of the many different types of four-holed cards available.

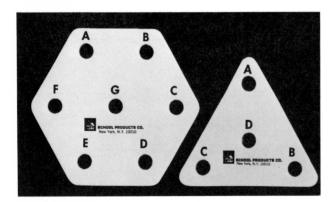

3-3. Not all cards have four holes; there are cards with three, six, and even eight holes. (School Products, New York)

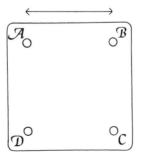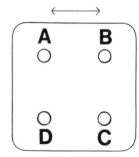

3-4. The nearer the holes are to each other, the narrower the shed will be.

BEATER

A beater is a device used to push the filling firmly into and against the opening of the warp. For card weaving, it must be narrow (in order to fit into the opening between the weaving and the cards) and have a firm edge.

Beaters made specifically for card weaving usually have a long handle to allow the weaver to enter the shed easily without getting a hand in the way. Other items can, however, be substituted. A likely item to use is a kitchen knife—not a sharp one that will slice into the weaving and possibly sever the warp from the weaving—but one with a dull bread-and-butter edge.

Another substitute can be found in the kitchen/gourmet department of most stores. It is a wood knifelike implement which has exactly the same shape as a beater made for card weaving. It is ideal—at one-fourth the price of one from a yarn store! A butter paddle is also ideal, with its tapered edge handle, and blunt end. A ruler with a beveled edge will do just as well, too. In fact, any straight edge—a strong piece of plastic or Masonite—is also adequate. In lieu of any special beater, extra cards themselves or the side of your hand can be used to beat against the warp.

SHUTTLE

A shuttle is a device on or around which the filling yarn is wound. It carries the filling through the opening of the warp ends from one side of the loom to the other. There are many styles of shuttles available in a weaving shop. The best type made for card weaving is the Norwegian belt shuttle, which has a tapered edge and notches for winding the filling yarn, and incorporates the function of the beater as well into its structure. The weaver can make a beater-cum-shuttle easily enough by simply cutting a piece of cardboard with slight indentations on the edges to allow for winding the yarn around it. (See Figure 3-7) If no shuttle is desired for holding the yarn (and some weavers prefer none), then a simple bobbin, ball of yarn, or butterfly can be used. The butterfly functions much the same way as a shuttle does—as a support for the yarn that is used as filling. The butterfly, however, has no wooden support onto which to wind the yarn. It is constructed over two fingers on your hand and is the simplest, most portable shuttle available.

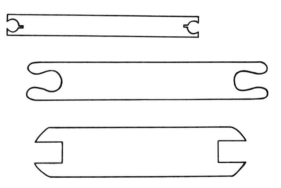

3-6. There are not quite as many common household substitutes for shuttles. These styles could, however, be copied out of cardboard or wood.

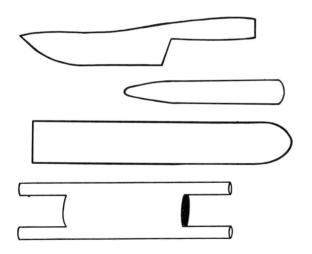

3-5. Beaters can be bought in many different shapes. Shown here from top to bottom: wooden kitchen utensil, bone or plastic style, wooden beater with tapered edge, and a replica of a very ancient style around the center of which yarn is wound.

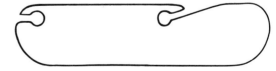

3-7. An example of the type of beater-cum-shuttle that is meant for card weaving. This shuttle conveniently releases yarn as needed and has a knife-like edge along the bottom which acts as a beater.

19

To make a butterfly, stretch your left hand out (if you are right-handed). If you want a large butterfly, you will use your pinky and thumb, and if you want a small butterfly, you will use your thumb and index finger. One end of the yarn is held securely between the index and middle fingers. Holding the two selected fingers up, wind the yarn around them in a figure 8, making the "X" or cross of the figure 8 on your palm. After winding enough yarn in this manner, make a slip knot with the loose end around the cross in the middle of the figure 8. Use the free end to feed the yarn through the shed and continue to pull yarn out of the butterfly as needed. (See Figure 3-8)

I generally prefer a butterfly or ball of yarn because it is more flexible than a shuttle and just as simple to use.

CLAMPS

These are necessary only if the weaver chooses to use some type of frame for weaving. (See Figures 3-9 and 3-10) Any ordinary clamp available at the hardware store is fine; it is used solely to secure the loom frame so that the weaver has tension against which to push and pull the cards, without having the loom jump up and down with each turn of the cards.

FRAME

Aside from the types of frame looms that you can build yourself with dowels and clamps, you can purchase a preconstructed frame loom, as the one illustrated in Figure 3-10. While these apparati facilitate some aspects of the weaving, they generally restrict the length of the warp that can be put up. It is difficult to maintain maximum tension on a frame loom when you pull the cards towards your body.

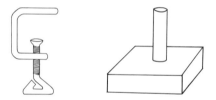

3-9. Dowels mounted on blocks of wood, secured to a table edge with clamps can be used to make a crude version of the loom featured in Figure 1-6.

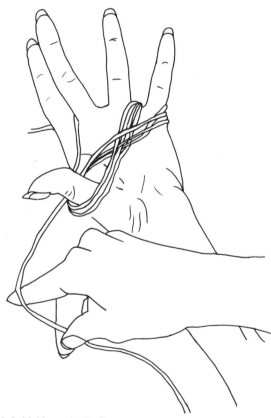

3-8. Making a butterfly.

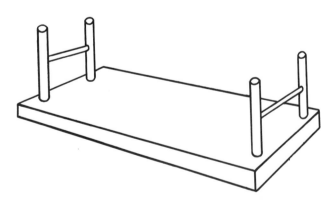

3-10. A more elaborate, but still simple, loom can be built easily with wood and dowels. This one is similar to the loom in Figure 2-7; both have front and back beams for the unwoven warp and completed weaving.

WAIST MATERIALS

These are things, obviously, at the weaver's waist (not to be confused with waste materials, of which there are many when weaving!). Instead of using a preconstructed frame, the weaver may choose to "build" a loom (as I do and recommend) and will, therefore, need a way to join the warp to either his chair or to himself. To do so, he can use a metal ring fastened at his waist, hooked onto his belt, or tied to a cord or scarf around his waist. A metal curtain ring, bangle bracelet, or meat-patty shaper are all ideal for this purpose. The weaver may alternately decide to tie the warp to a hanger, which he fastens to his waist. (Yes, a hanger!) The hanger should be made of wood—a flat, not round hanger—and the metal hook should be removed. Plastic (which would most likely snap under pressure) and metal (which would bend and also cut into the weaver's waist) are both inappropriate for card weaving. It is important that the hanger have little notches or grooves near its ends. A straight dowel can also be used, as illustrated on the jacket.

A cord with a loop knotted into each end is used to go around the waist and is attached to the hanger near its ends; the notches make "hitching posts" for the cord so that it does not slip off the hanger. The weaver who wishes the greatest comfort while working should pamper himself by indulging in a supersoft, maxi-padded hanger available in the closet or notion shop of department stores,

as well as in the five-and-ten-cent store. The weaver can easily cut indentations into this hanger. He can sew two tabs of Velcro (one at each end) on the hanger and sew the corresponding Velcro fastening tabs to the band or cord which he will use to circle his waist. A substantial card-woven band is practical for this purpose and could also be the first project you weave and put to practical use.

ASSORTMENT OF CORDS

Weavers always have bags and bags of scrap cords and stockpiles of miscellaneous leftovers or cut-offs from warps (the real waste materials!). If you are a new weaver, you would do well to start collecting. Cords of every sort and length could conceivably be used for something at sometime: strong, heavy-duty wrapping/packing cord; extra strength elastic bands; shoe laces; ponytail grips. The best of this assorted list is the ponytail fastener, available everywhere. This is a stretchy band, bound with a small metal closure, so that it won't pop open. It is coated with elastic fiber so it never catches the hair (and in this case, the warp), and holds securely. This strong tie is used to bind the warp ends together (discussed in Chapter 4).

These small cords are also used to bind the cards together to keep them from getting lost or jangled out of position. While threading the cards, a small string is used as a separating thread. While weaving, another piece of cord is used to secure the ring to the weaver's belt (or sash around his waist), or to connect the warp ends to the weaver's chair or to fasten a hanger around the weaver's waist.

Also in this category generically, but not functionally, is a scarf or strong, long tie, which is used to attach the loom—the end opposite the weaver—to a stationary object. (I use a one-inch-wide card-woven band, woven especially for this purpose; naturally, it is excellent for the job because of its strength and pliability.) A piece of packaging string, or a shoelace can be used. (The method of fastening is illustrated later in Chapter 4; see Figure 4-18)

MISCELLANEOUS

Scissors, masking tape, large tapestry needle, glue, measuring tape, ruler, pencil, and paper.

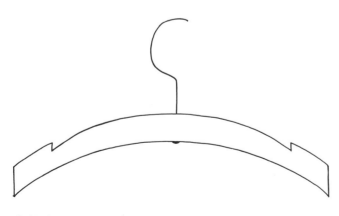

3-11. A wooden hanger such as this one with notches at each end is used to construct a simple type of loom.

FIBER

Almost any fiber can be used, but care should be exercised not to employ something that frays readily because the cards do rub the weaving. Furry or fuzzy materials such as mohair are not effective because they obscure not only the pattern, but also the beauty of the textured stitchery that is the hallmark of card weaving. They result in one long piece of fluff, discernible as neither card weaving, crochet, or knitting. All types of jute, although certainly strong enough, have a tendency to be hairy and, while they do not obscure the pattern as mohair does, they do produce belts

3-12. This detail of a Bulgarian belt shows how fuzzy and hairy coarse fibers (such as jute) become when woven. (Collection Hamburgisches Museum für Völkerkunde, Hamburg, Germany)

with a coarse texture. (See Figure 3-12) Although it has a lovely texture for crochet, chenille is not practical for card weaving because the little fibers which give it that plush, velvety look fall off all too easily with the turning of the cards. For fear of fraying, also, soutache (a flat strand of rayon over a cotton core) is not well suited, either. Both chenille and soutache can certainly be used (and I have, indeed, done so), but care should be taken while weaving.

Most other crochet threads are ideal and are readily available. Crochet threads are inexpensive and even come in novelty versions (that is to say, with gold and silver mixed in). Both perle and mercerized cottons are suitable. Cotton sewing threads may be used, but are not recommended because they are so fine and breakable.

All linens are perfect, as are all wools. Heavy-duty rug yarns are ideal because of their inherent body. Orlon tends to "fuzz up" with weaving, but I have never seen it shred and break. Combinations of wools and synthetics are good, too. Perlé (from France), one such synthetic (90% acrylic, 10% vinyon) is excellent. Aside from soutache, there are other rayon derivatives which work well: Rattail (a round fiber with body—woven rayon over cotton core), used often in macramé, is excellent, despite its "slippery" surface; chainnette (a chain-like, brightly colored thread), although it does not have the body that soutache does, is a joy to work with and has a lustrous finish that makes it look dressy; a thin filament known in the millinery trade as 6/3 twist creates resplendent work, and if this look is desired, it is well worth the care and labor required to work with a gossamer such as this; cordé (a round fiber with thin threads of rayon tendrilled around a cotton core) works easily into a pliant, rich fabric with a matte finish to it. Line braid (a flat braided fiber, available in widths of two-line, three-line and four-line) is not particularly good, as its flatness causes it to "stand-up" in the finished work.

All twisted cords, ropes, and macramé supplies may be used, as well as novelty threads, gold and silver Christmas ties, and all packaging strings. Thin velvet tubing (very expensive) produces a spectacular band—thick and luxuriant. Narrow (one-eighth-inch to one-quarter-inch-wide) double-faced satin ribbon also produces a rich-looking work, but the flat ribbon creates much the same problem as the flat line braid. (See Color Plates C-3 and C-18)

The card weaver should experiment with many fibers. Each has its advantages and disadvantages and each offers diversity of texture, width, thickness, pliability, etc. Combinations of different fibers can create not only interesting textures, but also enhanced patterns.

For beginning projects, it is wise to choose a relatively sleek fiber, because the cards will slide along it much more readily than with a wool or rougher texture. Textured fibers also require extra turning effort when weaving and greater patience when warping.

a

b

3-13. Line braid does not work well in a card-woven band because of its flatness (a). It is, however, becoming as an accent for texture when woven with another fiber (b). (See Pattern 17, where it is combined with rattail.)

4. Card Weaving Step-by-Step

SETTING UP

First, assemble all the necessary equipment on a flat surface. This grouping will vary, depending on the specific method chosen to weave. Most likely, you will need masking tape, scissors, yard-stick, measuring tape, ruler, shuttle and beater, paper, pencil, cards, miscellaneous strings, etc. All this equipment should be handy while you are threading the cards and weaving, to avoid unnecessary interruptions. Next, select the pattern you wish to use and keep it near by so you can refer to it for instructions.

READING A PATTERN

Card-weaving patterns are all practically self-explanatory. Most patterns are structured on grids, similar to the one shown in Figure 4-1, and are fairly standard. The numbers of the cards are listed across the top of the pattern draft, proceeding from right to left, as that is how the cards are arranged when weaving. The number of warp ends required is naturally four times the number of cards. The letters representing the holes in the cards (A, B, C, and D) are listed down the right-hand side of the draft (and sometimes down both sides) and the threading directions are given below the draft, along the bottom edge. An arrow ⟶ is front to back (F-to-B) threading; an arrow ⟋ is

back to front (B-to-F) threading. Each square will be lettered to indicate the color fiber that goes in that hole for a particular pattern.

With each of the pattern drafts in the following chapters all the necessary information is given in a paragraph below the draft. The warp fiber, filling, colors, and color distribution are all listed, as well as are the turning directions; it will soon become obvious that the basics of any design are the draft and the choice of color and fiber. In patterns where more than one color is used, a blank space is provided next to each color so that you may use this book to work from easily. Merely write in the color you are going to use, and you will have a handy workbook with a key for threading right next to each pattern.

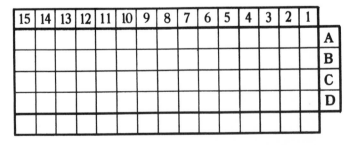

15	14	13	12	11	10	9	8	7	6	5	4	3	2	1	
															A
															B
															C
															D

4-1. A basic grid without color specifications for a fifteen-card draft.

24

Several groups of rudimentary patterns are presented in the next chapter. If you master the principles behind each set, you will have no trouble going on to more elaborate drafts. Moreover, learning to mentally translate a draft from paper to an image in your mind's eye is an important skill to develop.

From the pattern you have chosen, now count the number of cards required for the pattern and set them aside.

WARPING

Warping is the process whereby the fiber is cut into lengths (called warp ends) suitable for weaving. From your pattern you know the total number of warp ends you need (almost always four times the number of cards), and how many warp ends of each color are to be used. You must determine how long the warp should be cut.

For a first project, and until you get a feel for how much warp is necessary, it is a good idea to make the warp at least one-and-one-half times the length desired for the finished piece. Generally, a warp of about two-and-one-half to three yards is perfect for a sashed belt; somewhat less is enough for a belt with a buckle. In fact, if the fiber being used has little take-up (explained below), then a warp of one-and-three-quarter yards will just make it for a buckled belt. This is probably the least amount possible for a belt. For a pocketbook strap, a warp of one-and-one half yards is adequate. For double straps on a shoulder bag, a warp of four yards is necessary. A watchband requires only about eighteen inches. To make a potholder or a place mat, a long warp is necessary, as the finished band must be cut into sections and stitched together.

The length of the warp ends required depends on both the finished length of the item being woven and the amount of waste that will result during the weaving. Always allow for at least eighteen inches (and, more often than not, up to twenty-four inches) of waste on every pattern; that includes waste at both the beginning and the end of each warp end for the unweavable parts (because the cards get too close to the fastening to be turned), as well as those inches of warp which are totally wasted at both ends beyond the fastenings. This also allows for that amount of yarn lost in the weaving

through what is referred to as "take-up." In card weaving, it is the constant twisting action of the cards which causes a "shortening" of the warp ends. (On a regular loom, the take-up is in the weft or filling.)

When you work with a large number of cards and a heavy fiber, it is impossible to weave close to either end of the warp, and as much as a foot to eighteen inches may be wasted at each end. It may take many turns of the cards at the beginning of the weaving to get the band to its natural width, which is free from the "compressed" look that occurs at the onset of weaving; it may also require several turns (even up to twelve) to get the weaving action into a paced rhythm so that the selvages are even. You must consider these factors when deciding on what length to make the warp.

Once you have determined the length of the warp ends, you are ready to "put up" the warp. The warping procedures can be done by hand. That is to say, each warp end can be cut individually by measuring against a yardstick (or the like), or against another piece of fiber, already cut to size. Since most warps for card weaving are about two-and-one-half to three yards long, using a yardstick or another length of fiber as a measure would be cumbersome and time-consuming since most patterns require at least forty-eight warp ends. The inaccuracy that results makes these less than feasible methods. Furthermore, if any one warp end is cut shorter than the rest, the overall length of the weaving will be limited by that short warp end. It is, therefore, best to use either a warping board or an adjustable warping frame.

A warping board is a wooden frame (generally a yard long) with wooden pegs along its sides, around which the yarn is wound and measured. If a warping board is not available, then there are many substitutes around which to wind the fiber. Some possible household items to use include: chairs (either the backs, the arms, or the legs—turn the chair upside down on a table), doorknobs, dresser knobs, front beam of a floor loom, edge of a table, etc. (See Figures 4-2 to 4-5.)

Remember, you need two stationary objects to wind the yarn around; as with the butterfly, it is a good idea to make a figure 8 (or cross, as it is called in weaving) when you wind the yarn. This keeps the warp ends aligned, prevents snarling, and further enables you to count the warps should you lose track. (Count at the point of the cross, where the warp ends are neatly "stacked" up.)

A crude warping board can easily be constructed with a board and a few nails. A clamp can be used

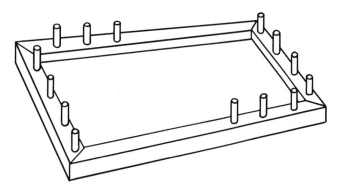

4-2. A warping board such as this is the most versatile and efficient means for putting up a warp. Any length of warp can be measured and cut by varying the pegs.

4-3. Warping around the front beam of a forty-five-inch loom and cutting the warp ends at one point gives a warp of two-and-one-half yards. The yarn is being fed from a ball in a fish bowl at the side of the loom—this keeps it clean as well as tangle-free.

to secure the board to a table to keep it stationary while working. As with all aspects of card weaving, ingenuity is the keynote to using what is available in the house.

If the warp needs to be two yards, then the ends of the warping structure must be either one or two yards apart. If they are one yard apart, then any piece of yarn that extends from one end of the warping structure to the other and then back again will be two yards long. If this is the case, after

4-4. Two chairs turned upside down on a table offer great variety as to the length of the warp put up. Here two different color yarns are being warped at the same time.

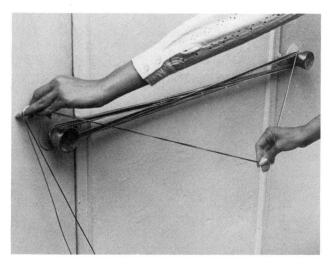

4-5. Two doorknobs eighteen inches apart are used for a short thirty-six-inch warp. Two different yarns are being warped together in the figure 8 style to facilitate counting.

measuring out the necessary amount of yarn, cut the warp at one point, and the resulting warp ends will be two yards long. If, for example, forty-eight warp ends (each two yards long) are needed, then forty-eight complete windings (from one end to the other and back again) would be required. If the warp is then cut at one point, forty-eight pieces of yarn, each of the same length (in this case, two yards), will be the result.

If the warping posts are two yards apart, then any one piece of yarn that stretches from one end to the other will, in fact, be two yards long. If the same forty-eight warp ends are needed, you need only make twenty-four complete windings. The warp is then cut at *two* places.

This is how to measure the warp ends when they are all of the same color yarn. When different amounts of different color warp ends are needed, they can either be warped separately (one color at a time), or together (all colors at the same time). If the second method is chosen, it is necessary to keep an exact count of the number of warp ends, starting with all colors that are going to be used. As you reach the desired number of warp ends for any particular color, simply drop that color off, and continue warping the rest until you reach the required number for another color group of warp ends.

PREPARATION FOR THREADING

The holes on most professionally manufactured cards are labelled on only one side (henceforth called the front side); to avoid errors while weaving, it is a good practice to label the holes on the backs of the cards as well before starting to thread them. Be certain when labelling the holes on the back sides of the cards that the letter at each hole corresponds to the letter on the front. Remember, the letters for the individual holes will not be in the same relative position on the backs of the cards as they are on the fronts. (See Figure 4-6) You may want to color-code the edges of the cards. You will be able to check the position of the cards faster by color than by letter. Color the edges of the corners near each hole with a different color crayon (for example, Aqua = A holes, Bright pink = B holes, Canary yellow = C holes, Dark green = D holes). For very complicated patterns with over

fifty cards, even the experienced weaver can benefit from color coding the corners of the cards.

Next, *number* the cards on both the front and the back. If the pattern selected calls for twenty-five cards, then take twenty-five cards and number them consecutively (in pencil) on the front and back, making sure that the numbers on the front and back of each card match. The numbers can always be erased when being used for other patterns, calling for different numbers of cards.

Threading directions will be given as a part of every pattern. Examine them. An arrow pointing up ↗ means back-to-front (B-to-F) threading and an arrow pointing down ↘ means front-to-back (F-to-B) threading. This is a fairly standard method of indicating threading procedures in card weaving. Some patterns call for total front-to-back or back-to-front threading, but most require a combination of the two.

Arrange the cards in the exact order called for by the pattern. For example: If F-to-B threading is indicated for Card 1, then place this card with the *front* side up, if F-to-B threading is also indicated for Card 2, then place that card also with the *front* side up, *below* Card 1. If Cards 3 and 4 both require B-to-F threading, then place them with the *back* sides up, *in numerical order* (i.e., Card 3 under Card 2 and Card 4 under Card 3).

In many cases, a pattern will call for half (generally the first half) of the cards to be threaded B-to-F and the other half to be threaded F-to-B. In cases such as these, it is practical to put the cards in two packets, each containing one-half of the total and have the first half face down and the second half face up, all *in numerical order*, naturally.

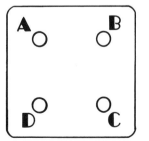 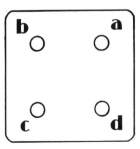

4-6. Left, the front of the card. Right, the back of the card.

Some other patterns call for threading in symmetrical pairs. This symmetrical threading is achieved by threading Card 1 B-to-F and Card 2 F-to-B. Card 3 is B-to-F, and Card 4 is F-to-B.

No matter what the threading schema, be certain to arrange the cards in numerical order, because threading instructions are listed that way. Do not divide the packet of cards in half and then turn one half face up and the other half face down—they will not be arranged numerically, which will cause complications later on. By taking the time before starting to thread the cards in proper order, you can save yourself time later, as well as errors that usually arise when threading a detailed pattern of forty or fifty cards.

Arrange the cut warp ends so that they are easy to reach and tangle-free. A good place to put them is over the back of a chair. If individual colors have been warped independently, then maintain their separateness by placing the different colored warp ends on opposite ends of the chair. If all the warp ends have been cut together, then do not bother to separate them by color into distinct bunches. When threading, extract the necessary color from the group as it is needed.

THREADING THE CARDS

Take the first card and note from the pattern what color warp ends go into which holes. You will find it convenient and probably make fewer errors if you hold the cards in your left hand between your thumb and index finger. The lettered side should be face up with the AD edge nearest your body.* An error in threading the colors as given in the pattern will result in a different design. Also note the direction in which each thread is inserted into the hole. If the cards have been arranged previously in the prescribed threading order, errors will be avoided at this point. An error in the direction of the threading matters greatly. Unless all four holes are threaded in the same direction, the card will never turn. If three warp ends are threaded properly, B-to-F, for example, and the fourth warp end is threaded F-to-B by accident,

*This is for front-to-back threading. For back-to-front threading—with the front of the card face down—the edge bearing the letters B-C should be nearest your body.

then the card will not turn when it is time to start weaving. In the beginning, at least, it is a good idea to double check each card against the threading directions. It is easier to correct an error in either the colors threaded or the direction of threading at this point than later when the loom is hooked up.

Holding the first card in your left hand, carefully direct each warp end into the proper hole. Accuracy is the most important aspect of this operation. (See Figure 4-7.) Be certain to have only six to eight inches of the warp ends go through the card to the other side.

Adjust the ends coming out of the holes in the cards so that they are all about the same length. Then, holding the short ends of the warp securely in your left hand, use your right hand to untangle the longer end of the warps if necessary. There will be a natural separation between the ends which are threaded through holes A and D and those which are threaded through holes B and C. Use your fingers to do this; do *not* use the card to slide up and down the warp ends.

When this operation is completed, place the front side of the card face down on the table, over the separating string. (See Figure 4-8) The separating string is mainly to keep the A and D warp ends separate from the B and C warp ends. It need not be so long as the warp ends themselves. A string twelve to fifteen inches long, preferably of a color different from the warp, so that it is visible and distinct, will do nicely. A thin fiber (such as a delicate linen) scarcely gets in the way and makes separation easy.

Pick up card number two, check the pattern instructions, thread the card, and lay it down on top of Card 1, again, with the front side face down. Be sure to keep the warp ends separated on the proper side of the separating string. Continue threading the entire pack of cards, and always place each card with its front side face down on top of the preceding card, unless specifically directed not to in the pattern instructions.

Pay particular attention to detail while threading. Try to keep: (1) The cards neatly stacked; (2) The four short warp ends on A-B side of cards even with each other and with those in all other cards; (3) The A and D ends separated from the B and C ends.

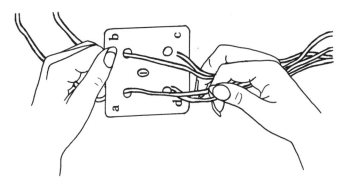

4-7. To thread a card F-to-B, hold the card in the left hand while directing the warp ends in the proper holes with the right hand.

4-8. This card is threaded F-to-B and turned face down over the separating string. Notice the natural separation between the warp ends threaded in holes A and D and those threaded in holes B and C.

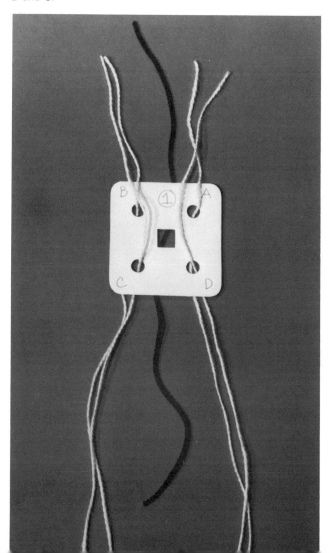

When the threading is completed, the very *first* thing to do is to tie the separating string around the packet of cards (Figure 4-10). At this point, before the actual weaving has begun, the separating string keeps the cards from slipping down the warp and becoming unthreaded. Tie the string firmly, but not so tightly that the cards cannot move at all. It is very important to get into the habit of tying the cards together with a separating string when not weaving.

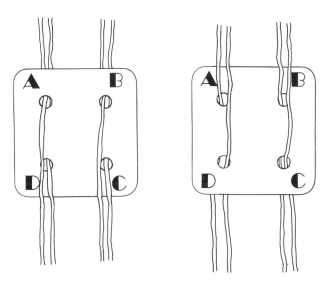

4-9. These two cards show the difference between F-to-B threading (left) and B-to-F threading (right).

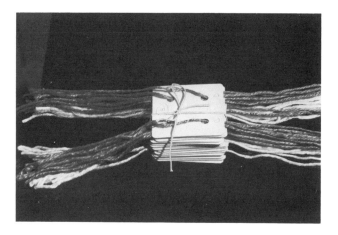

4-10. When all cards are threaded, the separating string is brought around the packet and tied securely.

FASTENING AND COMBING THE WARP

Now that the loom (remember, the cards *are* the loom) is "dressed," a structure must be created to support it. In order to be able to tie the dressed loom onto something, the warp ends must first be secured together at each end. To secure the short ends, grasp all the loose warp ends, and without tugging at any one end, band these ends together. For this task, I use a ponytail fastener (as discussed in Chapter 3). Be certain that: (1) all warp ends are included in the fastening, (2) the elastic is fastened as securely as possible, (3) no single warp end can slide out of the fastening.

Some weavers prefer to tie together each individual set of four warp ends from one card. This is easily done while threading. When the card is turned over and placed face down over the separating string, take the warp ends from holes A and D and tie them in a square knot to the warp ends from holes B and C. This method makes it very easy to deal with any warp end that is of a dissimilar length; as the double knot is tied, the weaver can control the length of all four warp ends to make them even. This method also enables the weaver to use as much of the warp as has been cut in order to waste as little as possible. Similarly, he can tie all four warp ends into one overhand knot. (See Figures 4-12a, b and 4-13a, b and the photograph on the front jacket flap.)

I prefer, however, to waste a little warp in order to save a lot of time, and fasten the entire bundle of warp ends with a ponytail fastener. Whatever fastening is used must be dependable, as it is most distressing to have warp ends fly out of their binding while weaving and most bothersome to have to keep resecuring them. If the warp ends are fastened properly, they need be fastened only once.

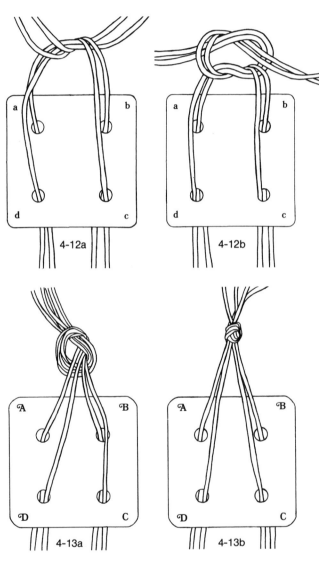

4-12, 4-13. Alternate methods of fastening the warp ends from each card together while threading: (4-12) a square knot, (4-13) an overhand knot. Be certain that these knots are tight and near the ends of the warps, so as not to waste much fiber.

4-11. The separating string is tied, and one end is being secured with an elastic ponytail fastener.

30

The fastener should be about three inches away from the ends and a similar distance from the cards. Be certain that all the warp ends are bound together—if one warp end is shorter than the others, it is likely that it will be omitted from the fastening. If this happens, the weaving will have to be interrupted and this binding procedure repeated to secure *all* the warp ends.

Similarly, if one warp end is longer than the others at this point, trace it through the elastic band and pull on it a little bit, until it reaches the length of the others. If it is very much longer on this end, then it will be commensurately shorter on the other end. By locating any short ends, you can gently pull them to make them the length of the other ends. The ends do not have to be *precisely* the same length; avoid, however, any ends that are several inches longer or shorter than the others.

Now that the short warp ends on the A-B side of the cards are tied, the long warp ends must also be fastened. In binding these ends together, the weaver must also insure that all the warp ends are of equal tension. To do that the cards must be pushed down the length of the warp. This requires the use of a firm (preferably stationary) object to which the fastened short ends can be tied, so as to be able to tug on the cards. Any stationary object will do: another person to hold the end, a paperweight or heavy pot placed on the cards, a doorknob or chair to which the end can be tied, etc. If the bound end of the warp is fastened to something higher or lower than waist height, the cards will be pulled down the warp at an angle, and the result will be uneven tension on the warp. For this particular task of combing the warp and fastening the other end, I use a window! It is ideal for many reasons, not the least of which is that it is waist level. A window is also strong. To secure the warp, open the window a little bit and place the bound end of the warp outside with the fastening point next to the frame. Be sure the *front* sides of the cards are to the *right*, with the edge bearing the A and D holes nearest the ceiling. Close the window; be certain that it closes near but not on the ponytail grip. That holds it firmly; forceful pulling on the cards will not dislodge the secured end. If the warp ends from each card have been knotted together, string a cord through all the loops formed by the four warp ends in each card, attach the cord to a stationary object, such as a doorknob, and begin combing.

Grasping the longer section of the warp at a point about two feet from the cards, start to unsnarl the ends gently. This is called "combing the warp." Carefully run your fingers through the warp to get out tangles and snags. If your fingers get caught at any point, work out the knot delicately, rather than by tugging at it. Combing the warp can be done with either both hands or one hand. Either keep one hand firmly on the warp ends and the other continuously combing, or alternate the position of your hands. While combing the warp, open the hand that is holding the warp to allow the excess to pass through. (See Figures 4-14 and 4-15)

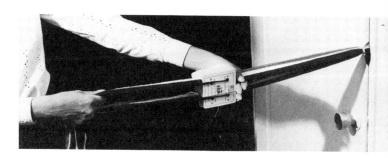

4-14. To start the process of combing, gently pull the cards down along the warp towards your body.

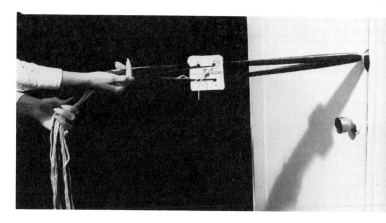

4-15. Comb the warp with the fingers of the right hand using an overhand motion alternated with an underhand direction. The left hand holds the warp ends firmly.

With Orlon, some wools, fibers that have little body, and thin fibers, there is always a tendency for the warp ends to cling to each other. Comb these warp ends gently, using extra care. Most rayon fibers (such as soutache and chainnette) rarely do this; in fact, rattail can be so "slippery" that the cards might even slide down the warp!

After combing about two feet of the warp, hold it securely with one hand and with the other grasp the cards on their edges (top A-D edge and bottom B-C edge). Sliding the cards down the warp may be difficult the first time, but after that it will be very easy. Placing your thumb on the top A-D edge of the cards, the pinky or fourth finger on the opposite B-C edge, and the other fingers on the far A-B edge (inside the opening formed in the warp ends), gingerly tug at the packet of cards to bring it toward yourself.

Slide the cards down to the point where you are holding the warp. Comb the warp for another two feet and repeat the process of moving the cards down the warp. The portion beyond the cards towards the window should be taut. Continue this process until you are six to eight inches away from the end. Grasp the warp securely, and fasten the end of the warp, just as you fastened the first end.

There is an alternate way of fastening this end. This second method wastes a lot more fiber than a simple elastic-band fastening, and doesn't really save any time, but for some weavers, it may be an easier method. This method requires the weaver to tie the entire set of warp ends together in an overhand knot, as shown in Figure 4-17. If you plan to tie the warp in this fashion, allow at least an extra six to eight inches when putting up the warp.

CONSTRUCTING THE LOOM

In looking for a stationary object onto which to fasten the loom, again consider only those objects which are about waist level. Because card weaving is generally executed while sitting, this height should be less than a yard off the ground. Possible stationary objects include: a doorknob, a hook in the wall, a table leg, or the open arm of a sofa. While traveling, the weaver must be imaginative to find something to hook on to. While at the beach, I have used balcony fencing; the arm or the leg of a chaise longue (provided someone is sitting in it to weight it); the leg of the lifeguard's stand; the wooden post to which the beach trash baskets are moored. In the backyard I have a favorite apple tree for this purpose. Naturally, you could keep the weaving secured in the window (providing that the sill will not get in the way as the weaving proceeds toward the window) if that is a convenient place.

The best way to fasten the weaving is with the aid of another band, scarf, or tie of some sort, threaded through the natural opening between the A-D and B-C warp ends and tied to the stationary object.

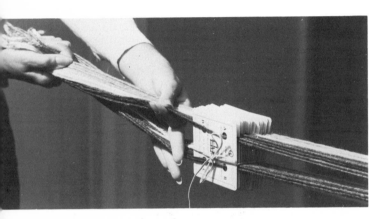

4-16. Comb almost the entire length of the warp. Do not go too close to the end, or the warp ends will slip out of your grip and out of the cards.

4-17. Fastening the other end of the warp with a firm overhand knot, as shown here, wastes a lot of warp—more than when fastened with an elastic band.

This allows flexibility and security at the same time. It is best not to tie the connecting band with a knot (or bow) in the middle of the warp ends; this would put undue stress on the warp ends and could ultimately cause them to become less taut in the areas over and under the tie. (See Figure 4-18.)

The other end of the loom is now ready to be fastened to the weaver's chair, another chair, or to the weaver himself. Just as in warping, inventiveness and personal comfort will dictate your choice.

To use the hanger method stretch the loom out from the doorknob to determine its length. The point where it ends is the place where your chair must go. Sit down and hold the outstretched warp in front of you. Insert the hanger through the triangular opening in the warp which is made by the edge of the cards and the tie. The warp will be perpendicular to the hanger. Gently tug at the hanger on both ends to be sure that all is secure. With a string or a band with loops at the end, secure the hanger around your waist. (See Figure 4-19.)

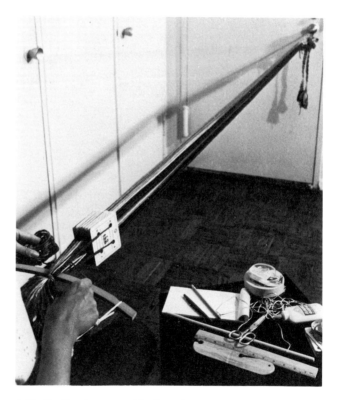

4-18. The end of the loom is fastened to the doorknob with a card-woven band. The bulky part at the bow is placed outside the warp, to avoid creating uneven tension in the warp ends.

4-19. Starting to weave. The loom is constructed, the hanger is inserted into the loom and hooked around the weaver's waist, and all necessary tools are directly at hand. The weaver is ready to turn the cards from the Home Position.

Now that your loom is set up note the position of the cards. The edge with the A and B holes should be further away from your body, the edge with the C and D holes, closest to your body; the edge near the ceiling has holes A and D in it, while the edge near the floor has holes B and C. The fronts of the cards should face right. This position is known as the Home Position and is *always* the starting and stopping position of all card weaving. All patterns start at this position unless a pattern *specifically* calls for something different. The weaver who learns always to leave the weaving in the Home Position will avoid careless errors later on when weaving complicated patterns.

Now push the chair back a little and feel the tension on the warp. Grasp the cards and feel the tension around them. Still holding the cards, slide them forward about six inches along the warp. Then, slide them back towards yourself. Look for irregularities in the warp. It is not uncommon for loose warp ends to appear at this time:

1. If a warp end is loose, it will loop toward the floor, and must be tightened. Very carefully trace it back to its origin and adjust its tension.

2. If it is very loose, it will fall to the floor. Carefully pick it up and determine from which end the fallen warp has come loose. Return it to that end, but without untying the fastening, simply secure it to the rest of the warp ends (*beyond the fastening*) with a piece of tape.

3. If it has become loose, fallen to the floor, *and* become unthreaded in the process of falling, then determine from which card the warp is missing. Rethread the card and secure the warp end to the proper end of the loom. Be certain, in rethreading, to *insert the warp end in the same direction as all the other warp ends in the card*.

LEARNING ABOUT THE LOOM

Remember it is the turning of the cards which causes the four warp ends in each card to twist over each other and become one; it is the addition of the filling which causes these twists to stay in place and results in a four-ply weave. (Three-holed cards produce a three-ply weave, six-holed cards produce a six-ply weave, etc.)

The addition of the filling is *through* the opening created between the warp ends which are threaded in the A and D holes and those in the B and C holes. This opening is known as the *shed* and it occurs as a natural separation. When the cards are turned, the shed is changed and a new shed is created. It is still formed by two distinct sets of warp ends; they are no longer, however, the warp ends which are from the A and D holes on the top edge and the B and C holes on the bottom edge. The warp ends which outline the new shed are in the same relative positions, but because the cards have been turned, new warp ends are in those positions.

The shed provides a place for the filling to settle in. After each shot of filling, the shed is changed by turning the cards. This action locks one shot of filling in place and also creates a new home for the next shot of filling.

In card weaving, two holes (and therefore, two sets of warp ends) are always "up" and two holes are always "down"; there is *always*, therefore, an open shed.

On a regular loom, the shed is also created by the placement of some warp ends up (as those in the A and D holes) and some warp ends down (as those in the B and C holes). This separation is achieved by activating levers or treadles which operate harnesses (corresponding to the cards) containing heddles (corresponding to the holes in the cards).

GETTING THE FEEL OF THE LOOM

Before you can turn the cards, you must remove the separating string that holds the cards together. Once this is untied, remember to keep the tension on the warp taut so that the cards remain aligned. To become familiar with the loom, you should first learn to slide the cards back and forth along the warp, since you will be doing this after *each* turn. As you will see when weaving, the sheds become entangled as a result of the changing positions of the warp ends. The forward shed must be cleaned to give the succeeding turn room to take place, and the back shed must be cleaned to minimize beating and to enable you to pack the previous shot of filling more easily.

To slide the cards toward you, place thumbs on the top A-D edge and index fingers inside the front shed. (An alternate method is to place index fingers outside the shed, one on top of the warp ends and one below.) Pull the cards, using the index fingers to exert pressure. (Figure 4-20a and b)

To push the cards away from you, place thumbs on the D-C edge of the cards, resting on the top of the warp outside the shed, index fingers at the B corners to guide them, third and fourth fingers along the bottom B-C edge of the cards, and pinkies at the C corners to guide them. Now push the cards forward along the warp with the thumbs.

In both the pushing and pulling actions, do not press the cards tightly together, or they will not move. Also do not ease up on the tension by leaning inward; you need a firm, tense warp *against* which to push and pull. Use a pulling/pushing movement before each turn. At first it may be difficult to maneuver the cards, but these operations will flow smoothly as one motion after a little practice.

Start a forward turn by exerting pressure at the D corner and pushing it downward away from you. Almost immediately, you will have to remove your index fingers from inside the shed, which is in the process of changing. When it opens up, it will be formed by different warp ends. As you do this, the D corner will be on top, with the cards at an angle. When the cards reach this angle, release your grip slightly to allow them to adjust to the new position— this is very important—and then replace the index and third fingers on the A-B edge, near B and the fourth and pinky fingers on the C-D edge, near C. With your index fingers, push the B corner toward you, rocking the cards gently. Work gingerly, but firmly, until you get the feeling of how to turn the cards. You will almost hear a "click" when the cards are turned correctly. After the packet of cards has been turned forward, slide them back and forth along the warp. There should be no resistance to their sliding; they should move along the warp just as easily as they did before they were turned.

After you have turned the cards forward, note the position of the lettered holes in the cards: D is where A was; C is where D was; B is where C was; A is where B was.

Slide the cards up and down along the warp to get the feel of changing their positions and, thereby, creating a new opening or shed. Then, holding the cards comfortably, turn them one turn back, toward yourself.

a.

b.

c.

4-20. It is important to use the pushing and pulling motions before and after each turn of the cards.

a. One method of pulling the cards toward you; index fingers in forward shed.

b. A second way to pull the cards toward you; index fingers outside far shed, above and below the warp ends.

c. Pushing the cards away from the weaving to clean the shed nearer your body.

35

To turn the cards backward, place your index and third fingers on the bottom (now A-B) edge of the cards. Place your fourth and pinky fingers along the back (B-C) edge, by the B hole, below the warp. With both thumbs on the C corner, push the cards down, while also pushing forward with your fourth fingers, which are at the B corner. When the D corner is up and the B corner down (the cards will then be at an angle), release your grip (as in the previous Forward turn), and move your thumbs to the D corner. Place third and fourth fingers at the B-C edge, and index fingers at B, along the A-B edge. Gently work the cards into their new position by moving thumbs along the A-D edge and pressing down, while using index or third fingers to push B up. Use pinkies to guide the bottom D-C edge of the cards. When the cards have been turned successfully, you will hear another "click." Push and pull the cards to clean the shed.

After one Forward and Backward turn, the cards will be returned to their Home Position. Note that four turns forward (each turn, rotating the cards 90 degrees) make one full cycle and return the cards to the Home Position, just as four turns backward make one complete cycle and also return the cards to the Home Position.

If at any time there seems to be trouble in turning the cards, determine which card is causing the problem. Check the four warp ends of the card and make sure that they are all threaded through the card in the same direction. If a card seems to be catching on itself, there probably is a warp end threaded incorrectly. Take the incorrectly threaded warp end out of the card and rethread it. Secure it to the rest of the warp ends or to the hanger with masking tape beyond the fastening.

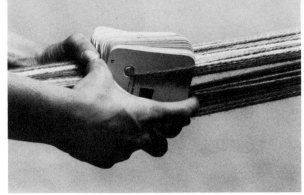

a.

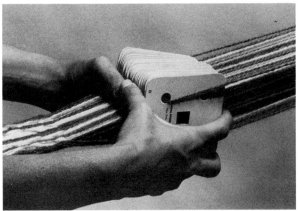

b.

c.

4-21. To make one forward turn and then one backward turn beginning at Home Position: (a) Start the turn by pushing all cards forward; (b) further forward motion to flip D corners up and put cards at an angle; (c) D corners being pressed down with the thumbs to finish turn (d). After the completed turn, notice the tangled warp where the index fingers are, as well as the new positon of the cards. (e) Pushing and (f) pulling the cards to clean the shed. (g) Continued pulling to lead into (h) backward turn, commencing by pressing the C corners down. (i) With C corners down as far as possible, release grip, adjust thumbs to press D corners down (j) to complete the backward turn (k).

36

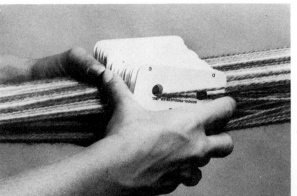

d.

e.

i.

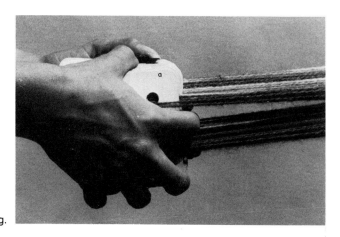

f.

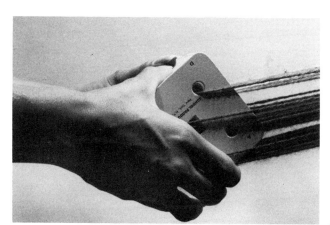

j.

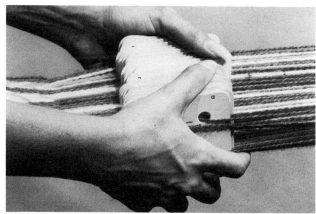

g.

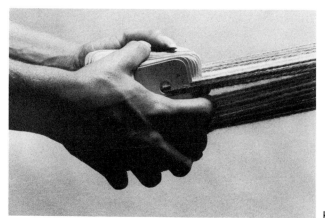

k.

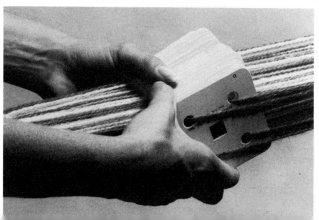

h.

37

WEAVING

First, select the color yarn that is to function as filling. (Remember, the filling scarcely shows at the edges and practically never shows on the face of the weaving.) If there is a solid border on the band, the color of the border is perfect for the filling. If the band is a solid, a contrasting color may look well showing through at the edges, as in Color Plate C-5 of a belt with a contrasting pink weft against a green border. Generally the filling material is the same as the warp fiber; in the case of a heavy yarn, it is better to select a thinner yarn for the filling. (See Color Plate C-3.)

After selecting the fiber to use as filling, wind the desired length (about a six- to eight-yard put-up is generally sufficient) on a shuttle, or into a ball or butterfly. When putting up the filling, you do not know how much is going to be needed. At least six to seven times the length of the warp is advised, but this is not always adequate. The amount of take-up varies with every fiber; the degree of tension varies with every weaver; the width of the band varies with the number of cards, also. Knowing how much to put up for the filling, then, is something that only experience can teach.

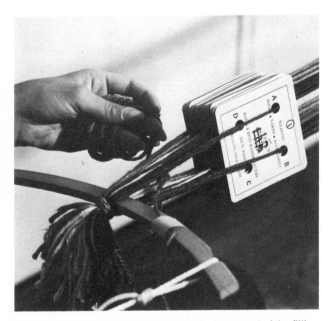

4-22. Before the weaving begins, tape the loose end of the filling to the hanger to secure it.

Hold the loose end on the right side of the warp and pass the yarn through the shed. Let it drop for the moment. To prevent the loose end on the right from flying about (as well as securing it so it will not be pulled through the shed), fasten it to the hanger with a bit of masking tape. Leave at least an additional six inches which will later be reworked back through the band to secure this free end of the filling.

Turn the cards one turn forward (1F). Using your beater, beat against the new shed, thus opening it neatly. Then, take the filling that is in your lap and pass it back through the new shed from left to right. Press it into the new shed, against the opening. Do not, however, pass it through so that it is tightly pressing up against the left edge of the weaving; leave a little slack on the edge. (See Figures 4-23a and b.)

The reason for leaving a little loop of filling on the edge of the band is twofold: First it affords you the opportunity to adjust the tension of the filling each time you turn the cards; secondly, and more importantly, it almost forces you to keep the tension even. It takes much practice to learn to keep both selvages neat and the width of the band equal throughout.

After the next turn forward, pull the filling to take up the slack. Then, feed the filling back (right to left), again leaving a little slack on the right side. Turn the cards forward and beat against the shed. Pull the filling to take up the slack. After four turns forward, the cards are returned to their original Home Position.

At this point, as a beginner, it is a good idea to check all the cards to be certain that none of them has slipped out of position. Be certain that all the A holes are in the same position, as should be all the B holes, C holes, and D holes. If you color-coded the edges of the cards (see Preparation for Threading) it will be easy to check the position of each card. As a practiced weaver, however, you will be able to tell immediately if there is an error simply by looking at the pattern emerging on the woven band.

Notice also that the warp at the far end of the loom is twisted. Since card weaving is really a process of twisting warp ends over each other, it is only natural that the warp should be twisted at the

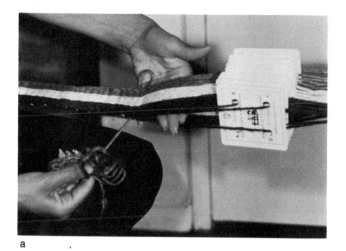

a

b

end without the filling. (Remember, the filling functions to keep the twistings in place.) To unravel those twists at the other end of the loom, simply weave a commensurate number of turns backward as woven forward.

Turning the cards backward (toward yourself) is the reverse process of weaving forward and nothing is changed except the manner of holding the cards to turn them. Continue to pass the filling through the shed and beat against the shed in the same fashion.

This untwisting process will naturally work whenever you weave the same number of turns forward and backward, regardless of whether the weaving pattern is eight turns forward and eight turns backward (8F / 8B), twelve turns forward and twelve turns backward (12F / 12B), etc.

The experienced weaver executing complicated designs may weave with very intricate turning patterns. As a beginner, however, it is wise to stick with multiples of four and variations of the four multiple—such as 4F / 2B / 4F / 2B / 2F / 4B / 2F / 4B. Even a turning pattern as relatively simple as this may require keeping a record of each turn on paper so as not to lose count.

4-23a, b. Leave a little slack with each shot of filling. This can be done by making a loop around your index finger.

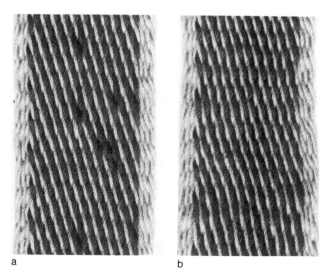

a   b

4-24a, b. Two parts of the same diagonal-stripe pattern on one band; notice how "bumpy" the stripe is in (a). This is a result of poor tension and uneven beating.

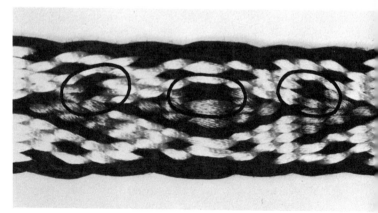

4-25. The circled areas reveal an apparent error in the symmetrical balance of this pattern. The bottom half is correct—the black outlines the medium tones against the light ground. The top half of the band, however, does not have that sharp black outline to define the design. The fifth card from the top edge has been threaded incorrectly—the black and the medium color were reversed.

The tangles at the far end of the loom will not necessarily be removed—if a pattern calls for all forward turns, all backward turns, or a dissimilar number of forward and backward turns, twists will accumulate at the far end of the warp. It is impossible to weave once you have "caught up" to these spiralled warp ends. You can push them forward toward the far end of the loom every so often to allow maximum weaving room, but eventually they will have to be removed. To do so, unfasten the warp at the far end, remove the twists, gently comb through the warp, refasten the end (being certain that all warp ends have an equal tension), secure the end of the loom to its post, and continue weaving.

The point where you reverse the direction in which the cards are turned is called a turn reversal. The turn reversal is comprised of a long, straight stitch that does not slant in any direction, unlike the rows of stitches before and after it. *In all cases* the direction of the slant of the stitches *changes* at the point of the turn reversal. Furthermore, on a patterned band at the point of the turn reversal, the pattern seems to stop and symmetrically repeat itself. If you want to see how a pattern will look when reversed, place a mirror flush against the last row of completed weaving just before you are about to change the turning direction. The reverse image shown in the mirror is exactly the printout of the band that the turn reversal will render including the change in the slant of the stitches. This is an important aspect and a basic property of card weaving.

Being able to recognize turn reversals will help you determine where you are in a turning sequence. There are two distinct formations possible along the rib of a turn reversal and they are solely a function of the threading of the cards. If all the cards are threaded in the same direction, then every reversal looks the same—straight stitches across the width of the band a little longer than the other rows of stitching.

When adjacent cards are threaded in *opposite* directions, however, the turn reversal manifests itself in two distinct ways. Now look at Figure 4-26. Beginning at the left of the photograph, the first, fourth, seventh, and tenth rows of weaving are turn reversals, recognizable by their *long* rows of straight stitches. The two adjacent cards in the center of this band were threaded in opposite directions. In the center of the first and third turn reversals, you will see two warp ends that are very close together and appear to be a single stitch. In the center of the second and fourth turn reversals you will see a little opening where the filling shows through. If you were to turn this band over, you would see that the first and third turn reversals on that side look the same as the second and fourth reversals on the top of the band—a little opening where the filling shows through—and the second and fourth reversals on that side look like the first and third reversals on the top of the band—two warp ends that form a single stitch. When the turning direction is changed, one of these two formations will result at every point along the width of the band where adjacent cards are threaded in opposite directions. These two forms of the turn reversal alternate as the weaving proceeds. A detailed explanation of turn reversals and their technical development can be found in Chapter 9.

Being able to recognize a turn reversal will help you avoid likely pitfalls. Two of the most common errors in card weaving occur while threading and turning the cards. A mistake in the former will generally be quite noticeable. Since each card is responsible for only one stitch in each row of weaving across the width of the band, an error (the misthreading of an entire card or the inaccurate placement of different colored warp ends in a single card)

4-26. The raised ribs on the surface of the band, actually "longer stitches" appearing at regular intervals, are turn reversals. At every other one, the filling shows through on the surface.

will surface in the improper execution of the design. (See Figure 4-25.) A mistake in turning, however, can be much more subtle and is often difficult to detect, because the entire length of the woven band is not in front of you. (See Figure 4-27.)

If you suspect that you have made an error, or, if you forget where you are in a turning sequence, you should first scrutinize the entire length of the band for visible mistakes. Look at the overall pattern, coloration, and angle of the stitches and then count the rows of weaving from the turn reversal.

If you forget whether you are in a sequence of forward or backward turns, make a simple test. For example: you return to your weaving to find the C-B edge of the card on top (C in the far corner, near the doorknob and B near your body) and you do not remember whether you are in the middle of a series of forward or backward turns. The pattern you are weaving calls for 12F / 12B. To test where you are, simply turn the cards one turn forward. Do *not* feed the filling through during this test. If the shed opens up and releases the previous shot of filling, then you know that you were *not* weaving forward. Go back to the original position before the test, feed the filling through, and continue weaving, *backward*. If, however, after the forward test turn, the shed does not "open up" and release the filling, then you know that you *were*, in fact, weaving forward. Return to the test position, feed the filling through, and continue to weave forward.

If you can recognize a turn reversal, there is another very simple test you can make to determine in which direction the cards were last turned: Weave two turns forward to see whether the long straight stitch of the turn reversal occurs. If it does not, then you know that the weaving that preceeded this test was also Forward. If, however, the two test turns produce a turn reversal, then you know that you were *not* weaving Forward.

If, after determining that you ought to be weaving forward, you do not know how many forward turns you must do to complete the cycle, (in the same 12F / 12B pattern), then you must look at the weaving and count the stitches (turns) from the point of the last turn reversal. If, from the turn reversal, you can determine that you have already woven six forward turns, then you know that you

have to weave six more turns forward before you can reverse the direction of the weave. (Count the long stitch of the turn reversal itself as two stitches, for it actually takes the place of two short stitches. Why this is so is explained in Chapter 9.)

If you are working with a pattern requiring all turns in the same direction, the weaving will proceed very rapidly, as there is little to complicate the mechanical process. When the woven section of the band gets to such a point that it is hard to reach the cards beyond it, then it is time to adjust your position. If you are sitting on a chair next to the loom (with the loom supported on two stationary objects) then simply move your chair to the point where the cards are so that they are comfortably within your reach. If you are weaving with the loom attached to the side of the chair on which you are sitting, then release the band and refasten it at a point nearer the cards. Never overreach your grasp to turn the cards; this has a tendency to slacken the warp tension and thereby increase the width of the band.

If the weaving is attached to a ring at your waist, use safety pins to attach it at another point along the band, closer to the cards. If you are using the hanger method, then roll the weaving up around the hanger and replace it around your waist. (See Figure 4-27.) If the warp ends have been secured with a ponytail fastener, then rolling the completed weaving around the hanger (and, thus, over this lumpy bunch of warp ends) will produce uneven tension on the outstretched warp. To alleviate this

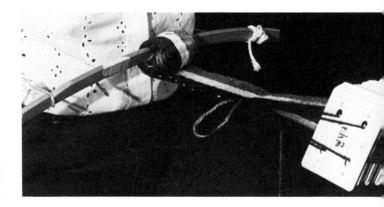

4-27. Winding the woven section of the band around the hanger is the simplest solution to the problem of what to do with the weaving when it gets out of reach.

problem, stuff some cotton or pieces of yarn in the "hollows" as you spool the weaving around the hanger.

Generally, it will take about eight turns before the cards settle into a comfortable position. They will be too close to each other in the beginning and sometimes even more than eight turns will be necessary in order for them to spread out. You will be able to tell when you have reached an even rhythm of turning and thereby attained the maximum width from the cards and fiber. Often the use of a "heading" is advisable to get the cards to spread out; when a heading is used it takes fewer turns for the cards to get to their natural width than it does when weaving with a narrow filling.

This means starting the weaving with a filling heavier than the one intended for the weaving—and, in fact, the heavier the better. If a very large number of cards is being used, it will be necessary to use a heading made out of slats of strong cardboard—one inch wide and several inches longer than the anticipated width of the band. As many as eight of these may be needed for "filling" until the band spreads out. After the band is finished, the heading may be removed; generally, it will have wasted several inches of warp and that factor must be considered when determining the length of warp required.

Always remember to tie the packet of cards together with the separating string when leaving the weaving for any amount of time, because it is very easy for the cards to jangle out of position. After the cards have been tied together, push them back against the last row of completed weaving. This keeps the weaving secure and prevents the cards from sliding. A good way to leave the loom is shown in Figure 4-28. The warp can be wrapped around the hanger and put into a bag for storage or traveling.

A problem may occur as weaving continues: running out of filling. It cannot always be anticipated—but sometimes it is actually planned! When you see that the filling is about to run out, start to add a new piece. Generally, it is time to add a new piece when there is about three times as much filling left as the width of the band. That is to say, if the band is two inches wide, start to add a new piece of filling when there are six inches left of the

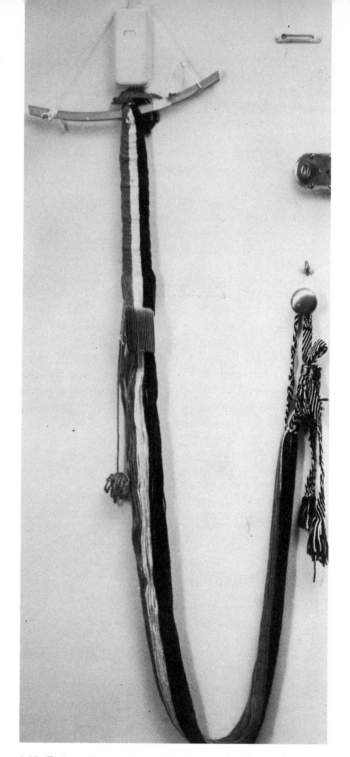

4-28. To keep the weaving and the loom out of the way when not being used, simply hang it up. If the unwoven section of the warp is too long and drags, then wrap the woven portion around the hanger, which also helps keep the loom as compact as possible.

old filling. If the band is five inches wide, then start to add a new piece of filling when the old filling has fifteen inches left. It is always better to overlap the two fillings for two or three shots—if one of the ends of filling starts to unravel, there is then another bound in the weaving to keep it secure.

It is a wise idea when doubling the filling to have the new filling go through the shed in the direction *opposite* the old filling. If the old filling is going through from left to right, then start the new filling feeding through the shed from right to left. After three or so doubled shots, drop off the old filling (if there is any left) and continue weaving with the new filling. The two loose ends of the filling can be reworked back into the weaving later on with the aid of a tapestry needle.

As you approach the end of the warp, the bulk of the woven band will be wrapped around the hanger and there will be very little warp left to weave. Try to complete the weaving at a point which ends a turning sequence. When you can no longer weave, put the separating string around the cards and feed the filling through the open shed, even though you are not going to close the shed by turning the cards. Do not leave any slack in the filling, but rather pull it all the way through the open shed firmly and then bring it around to the front of the band. Fasten it there with either a pin or masking tape, leaving at least six inches of excess filling on this end, as you did with the other end.

Remove the weaving from the doorknob, undo the elastic at the end, untie the separating string, and remove the cards. At the near end, remove the tape (which was used to secure the beginning of the weaving to the hanger), and attach the loose end of the filling to the face of the weaving. Slide the hanger out of the weaving, and undo the elastic band.

That is all there is to card weaving. Once you have tried it, you will see that it is easier than it sounds, and infinitely varied.

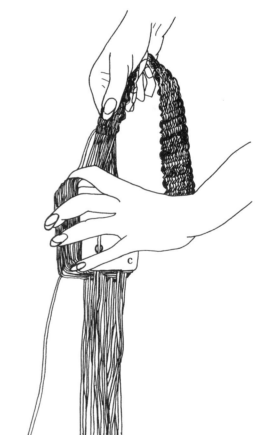

4-29, 4-30. After removing the loom from the doorknob unfasten the elastic band. Notice all the twists in the warp ends—a result of weaving in one direction. Comb out the tangles and then firmly grasp the pack of cards in one hand and the woven band in the other and pull the cards down off the warp ends.

5. The Basic Weaves

SOLIDS

It sounds incorrect to describe drafts for solid-colored bands as patterns, because they clearly do not produce designs. They do, however, constitute a distinct pattern type, and it is this model which the weaver should learn to recognize. (Figure 5-1 illustrates the basic pattern draft for the solid weave.)

This is not very hard to understand. Since a single-colored weave results, it is obvious that only one color was used in the warp. That means that all four warp ends in each card are the same.

The discussion here is confined to bands which are true solids—woven with the same fiber in each hole of every card. This is to acquaint the student with the basics on which to build and to familiarize him with the varieties of solids that can be achieved through variations in threading and turning the cards.

All solid patterns do not have to be boring. Variegated yarns add interest to solids with their irregularities of color placement. There are times when a solid is desirable and even a tiny solid band can be practical in the proper place—for example, see the watchband in Figure 1-1, which is made from navy blue linen.

5-1. Model twenty-card draft for solid bands.

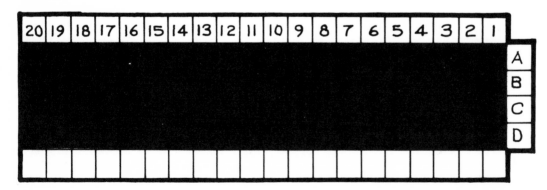

44

Key points to remember:
- All holes in all cards are threaded with the same fiber.
- To achieve variety, change the threading direction of individual or groups of cards.
- For further diversity, alternate turning sequences.
- All four warp ends in any given card must be threaded in the same direction or the card will not turn.

Pattern 1
Warp Fiber: Mercerized, two-ply cotton
Filling Fiber: Same as warp
Warp Ends: 60 Green (variegated)
Turning: All Forward

For a first try, this pattern is purposely simple—all 60 warp ends are threaded in the same direction and the cards are turned in the same direction. A green variegated cotton was chosen in order to give some variety to a solid pattern.

When finished, let the piece hang freely. You will notice that it has a tendency to spiral. This is often true of bands which are woven entirely in one direction. This twisting tendency can easily be stopped by steaming the belt in several ways: with a steam iron for hardy fabrics, by hanging the weaving in a steamed-up bathroom, or by holding it over a pot of boiling water (both of the latter methods work well with delicate fabrics).

The fact that the number of cards is uneven does not matter. An uneven number of cards is often the basis for a pattern.

15	14	13	12	11	10	9	8	7	6	5	4	3	2	1
G	G	G	G	G	G	G	G	G	G	G	G	G	G	G	A
G	G	G	G	G	G	G	G	G	G	G	G	G	G	G	B
G	G	G	G	G	G	G	G	G	G	G	G	G	G	G	C
G	G	G	G	G	G	G	G	G	G	G	G	G	G	G	D
↖	↖	↖	↖	↖	↖	↖	↖	↖	↖	↖	↖	↖	↖	↖

5-2a, b. Draft and band, Pattern 1.

45

Pattern 2

Warp Fiber: Four-ply Orlon
Filling Fiber: Same as warp
Warp Ends: 80 Pastels (multi-colored/variegated)
Turning: All Forward

This pattern is a variation of Pattern 1. In this case symmetrical threading has been introduced. Notice that half the cards are threaded B-to-F and the other half are threaded F-to-B. This difference is apparent in the direction of the "stitches": In Pattern 1 the stitches all slant in the same direction; here they slant in two directions, toward the center.

5-3a, b. Draft and band, Pattern 2.

20	19	18	17	16	15	14	13	12	11	10	9	8	7	6	5	4	3	2	1	
P	P	P	P	P	P	P	P	P	P	P	P	P	P	P	P	P	P	P	P	A
P	P	P	P	P	P	P	P	P	P	P	P	P	P	P	P	P	P	P	P	B
P	P	P	P	P	P	P	P	P	P	P	P	P	P	P	P	P	P	P	P	C
P	P	P	P	P	P	P	P	P	P	P	P	P	P	P	P	P	P	P	P	D
↖	↖	↖	↖	↖	↖	↖	↖	↖	↖	↗	↗	↗	↗	↗	↗	↗	↗	↗	↗	

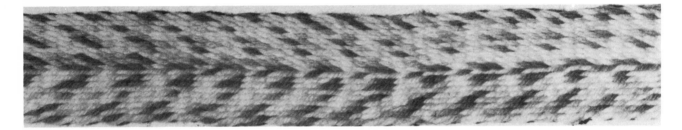

Pattern 3

Warp Fiber: Thin rattail
Filling Fiber: Same as warp
Warp Ends: 44 Black
Turning: 4F / 4B

This pattern introduces another building technique—the turn reversal. Notice that the ribs on the band mark the points at which these reversals occur. The size of the stitch is changed which adds an attractive, new dimension.

11	10	9	8	7	6	5	4	3	2	1	
B	B	B	B	B	B	B	B	B	B	B	A
B	B	B	B	B	B	B	B	B	B	B	B
B	B	B	B	B	B	B	B	B	B	B	C
B	B	B	B	B	B	B	B	B	B	B	D
↖	↖	↖	↖	↖	↖	↖	↖	↖	↖	↖	

5-4a, b. Draft and band, Pattern 3.

Pattern 4

Warp Fiber: ¼" double-faced satin ribbon
Filling Fiber: Thin rayon (white)
Warp Ends: 40 White
Turning: 16F / 16B

This experiment with satin ribbon was most successful—for a solid band. (See Color Plate C-18.) For a patterned design this type of flat ribbon would be less suitable. A band such as this would make an elegant strap for an evening bag. Notice the detail of this weave: It is a solid weave with indistinct rows.

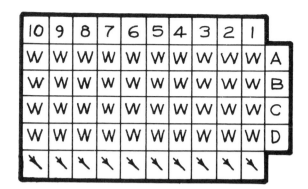

10	9	8	7	6	5	4	3	2	1	
W	W	W	W	W	W	W	W	W	W	A
W	W	W	W	W	W	W	W	W	W	B
W	W	W	W	W	W	W	W	W	W	C
W	W	W	W	W	W	W	W	W	W	D
↘	↘	↘	↘	↘	↘	↘	↘	↘	↘	

5-5a, b. Draft and band, Pattern 4.

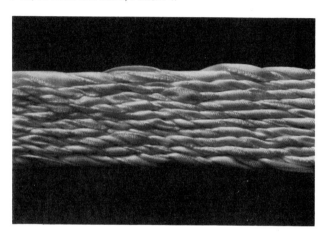

Pattern 5

Warp Fiber: Lightweight soutache
Filling Fiber: Same as warp
Warp Ends: 56 Pink
Turning: 4F / 4B

Notice the results achieved with soutache. Although it is a flat fiber, like the satin ribbon used in Pattern 4, it does not result in a tight weave; it is loose, and seems to have "holes." This is the first pattern presented with both standard turning (4F / 4B) and symmetrical threading.

14	13	12	11	10	9	8	7	6	5	4	3	2	1	
P	P	P	P	P	P	P	P	P	P	P	P	P	P	A
P	P	P	P	P	P	P	P	P	P	P	P	P	P	B
P	P	P	P	P	P	P	P	P	P	P	P	P	P	C
P	P	P	P	P	P	P	P	P	P	P	P	P	P	D
↘	↘	↘	↘	↘	↘	↘	↗	↗	↗	↗	↗	↗	↗	

5-6a, b. Draft and band, Pattern 5.

Pattern 6

Warp Fiber: Thin rattail
Filling Fiber: Thin rattail (a shade slightly differ-
ent from the warp color)
Warp Ends: 60 Rust
Turning: 4F / 4B

A different color filling was used here, but the difference in color is so slight that it does not show at the edges in an unattractive way. (See Color Plate C-14.) See if you can see the filling showing through at the turn reversals.

15	14	13	12	11	10	9	8	7	6	5	4	3	2	1	
R	R	R	R	R	R	R	R	R	R	R	R	R	R	R	A
R	R	R	R	R	R	R	R	R	R	R	R	R	R	R	B
R	R	R	R	R	R	R	R	R	R	R	R	R	R	R	C
R	R	R	R	R	R	R	R	R	R	R	R	R	R	R	D
✓	✓	✓	✓	✓	✓	✓	↖	↖	↖	↖	↖	↖	↖	↖	

5-7a, b. Draft and band, Pattern 6.

Pattern 7

Warp Fiber: Thin rattail
Filling Fiber: Same as warp
Warp Ends: 52 Navy blue
Turning: 12F / 12B

Compare this band to Pattern 6, which is woven 4F / 4B. This pattern (with 12F / 12B) appears to be in a checkerboard design, even though it is of only one color. This is due to the nature of the rattail. Pattern 6 does not have the color-shaded blocks that Pattern 7 has because the turn reversals occur more often in the former.

13	12	11	10	9	8	7	6	5	4	3	2	1	
N	N	N	N	N	N	N	N	N	N	N	N	N	A
N	N	N	N	N	N	N	N	N	N	N	N	N	B
N	N	N	N	N	N	N	N	N	N	N	N	N	C
N	N	N	N	N	N	N	N	N	N	N	N	N	D
✓	✓	✓	✓	✓	✓	↖	↖	↖	↖	↖	↖	↖	

5-8a, b. Draft and band, Pattern 7.

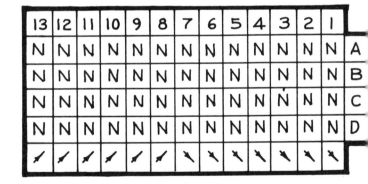

HORIZONTAL STRIPES

In order to get a horizontal stripe (a stripe that runs the length of the weaving not its width), all four holes of any one card *must* be threaded with the same color. Below is the basic pattern draft for twenty cards for a horizontal stripe. The odd-numbered cards are one color, while the even-numbered cards are another color. This causes each line of weaving to be one color. These alternating rows of color produce the stripes.

Key points to remember:
- "Horizontal" refers to a stripe down the length of the band.
- All four holes of any individual card *must* be threaded with the same color.
- A change in the turning directions will not affect the stripe, merely the direction of the slant of the stitch.

5-9. Model twenty-card draft for horizontal stripes.

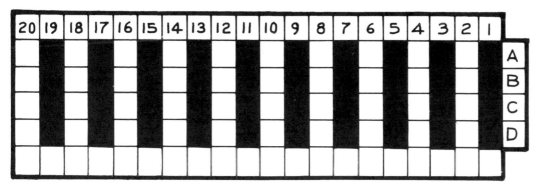

20	19	18	17	16	15	14	13	12	11	10	9	8	7	6	5	4	3	2	1	
																				A
																				B
																				C
																				D

Pattern 8

Warp Fiber: Three-ply rug yarn (75% rayon, 25% cotton)
Filling Fiber: Same as warp
Warp Ends: 72
Warp Breakdown: 24 Green
24 Rose
24 Brown
Turning: All Forward

This heavy-duty yarn is surprisingly easy to work with. The finished weaving is ideal for a potholder (or several potholders, cut to size) because it is thick, yet pliable.

5-10a, b. Draft and band, Pattern 8.

18	17	16	15	14	13	12	11	10	9	8	7	6	5	4	3	2	1	
R	R	R	B	B	B	G	G	G	R	R	B	B	G	G	R	B	G	A
R	R	R	B	B	B	G	G	G	R	R	B	B	G	G	R	B	G	B
R	R	R	B	B	B	G	G	G	R	R	B	B	G	G	R	B	G	C
R	R	R	B	B	B	G	G	G	R	R	B	B	G	G	R	B	G	D
↘	↘	↘	↘	↘	↘	↘	↘	↘	↘	↘	↘	↘	↘	↘	↘	↘	↘	

Pattern 9

Warp Fiber: Four-ply "Speed-Cro-Sheen" cotton
Filling Fiber: Same as warp
Warp Ends: 48
Warp Breakdown: 24 Brown
                         16 Red
                          8 Pink
Turning: All Forward

In this instance, half the warp is threaded B-to-F and the other half is threaded F-to-B, unlike the stripe in Pattern 8. With stripes as these, the threading does not matter nearly so much as it does with diagonal stripes, discussed later.

12	11	10	9	8	7	6	5	4	3	2	1	
R	B	R	B	P	B	B	P	B	R	B	R	A
R	B	R	B	P	B	B	P	B	R	B	R	B
R	B	R	B	P	B	B	P	B	R	B	R	C
R	B	R	B	P	B	B	P	B	R	B	R	D
↖	↖	↖	↖	↖	↖	↗	↗	↗	↗	↗	↗	

5-11a, b. Draft and band, Pattern 9.

Pattern 10

Warp Fiber: Heavy-weight rattail
Filling Fiber: Lightweight rattail (navy blue)
Warp Ends: 44
Warp Breakdown: 24 Navy blue
                         16 Light blue
                          4 Green
Turning: 16F / 16B

At the point of the turn reversal, the rib breaks the rhythm of the weaving and results in a longer stitch. This pattern is shown in Color Plate C-7.

Pattern 11

Warp Fiber: "Wintuk," a two-ply Orlon
Filling Fiber: Same as warp (green)
Warp Ends: 72
Warp Breakdown: 48 Green
                         24 Blue
Turning: 12F / 12B

This is but one of the many possible varieties of the horizontal stripe. Rows of blue and green striping could be added in different widths to this band as desired.

Pattern 12

Warp Fiber: Three-ply Orlon
Filling Fiber: Same as warp (blue)
Warp Ends: 40
Warp Breakdown: 20 White
                         20 Blue
Turning: All Forward

Notice that this band of stripes is not threaded in overall symmetry, but rather in symmetrical *pairs*. The overall effect is different from that achieved in Pattern 9, where the symmetry is based on the whole band, not on pairs. This same pattern is shown woven from rattail in Figure 5-14c.

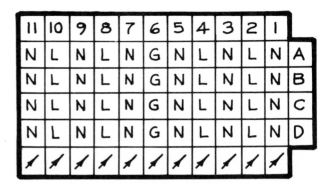

11	10	9	8	7	6	5	4	3	2	1	
N	L	N	L	N	G	N	L	N	L	N	A
N	L	N	L	N	G	N	L	N	L	N	B
N	L	N	L	N	G	N	L	N	L	N	C
N	L	N	L	N	G	N	L	N	L	N	D
↗	↗	↗	↗	↗	↗	↗	↗	↗	↗	↗	

5-12. Draft for pattern 10.

18	17	16	15	14	13	12	11	10	9	8	7	6	5	4	3	2	1	
G	G	G	G	G	G	B	B	B	B	B	B	G	G	G	G	G	G	A
G	G	G	G	G	G	B	B	B	B	B	B	G	G	G	G	G	G	B
G	G	G	G	G	G	B	B	B	B	B	B	G	G	G	G	G	G	C
G	G	G	G	G	G	B	B	B	B	B	B	G	G	G	G	G	G	D
↘	↘	↘	↘	↘	↘	↘	↘	↘	↗	↗	↗	↗	↗	↗	↗	↗	↗	

5-13a, b. Draft and band, Pattern 11.

10	9	8	7	6	5	4	3	2	1	
B	W	B	W	B	W	B	W	B	W	A
B	W	B	W	B	W	B	W	B	W	B
B	W	B	W	B	W	B	W	B	W	C
B	W	B	W	B	W	B	W	B	W	D
↘	↗	↘	↗	↘	↗	↘	↗	↘	↗	

5-14. Pattern 12. (a) Draft, (b) band woven in Orlon and, (c) in rattail.

VERTICAL STRIPES

There is a similarity among vertical-stripe patterns (stripes that run the width of the weaving, not its length) just as there is with horizontal-stripe patterns. The vertical stripe results from threading all the A holes in every card with the same color warp end, all the B holes with one color, the C holes with one color, and, of course, all the D holes with one color.

The basic pattern draft for vertical stripes is shown below.

Key points to remember:

- "Vertical" refers to a stripe across the width of a band.
- All corresponding holes across the band *must* be threaded with the same color which is going to produce the stripe.
- Threading can be varied but for neatest results thread the cards all in one direction, or half F-to-B and half B-to-F.
- Turning directions will affect the printout of the stripes.

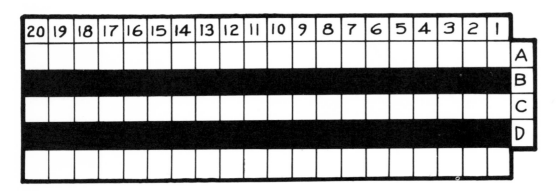

5-15. Model twenty-card draft for vertical stripes.

Pattern 13
Warp Fiber: Thin rattail
Filling Fiber: Same as warp (red)
Warp Ends: 40
Warp Breakdown: 20 Blue
⠀⠀⠀⠀⠀⠀⠀⠀⠀⠀ 20 Red
Turning: 4F / 4B

Notice how the width of the stripe increases at the point of the turn reversal.

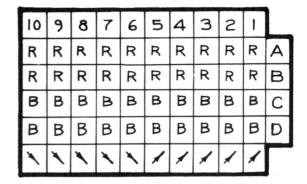

5-16a, b. Draft and band, Pattern 13.

Pattern 14

Warp Fiber: Two-ply heavy rayon rope
Filling Fiber: Thin cotton (pink)
Warp Ends: 48
Warp Breakdown: 24 White
                     12 Pink
                     12 Black
Turning: All Forward

This is a heavy fiber, and the band is ideal for jobs that require extra strength—suitcase grips, for example.

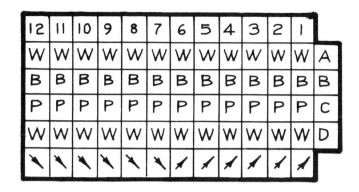

12	11	10	9	8	7	6	5	4	3	2	1	
W	W	W	W	W	W	W	W	W	W	W	W	A
B	B	B	B	B	B	B	B	B	B	B	B	B
P	P	P	P	P	P	P	P	P	P	P	P	C
W	W	W	W	W	W	W	W	W	W	W	W	D
↖	↖	↖	↖	↖	↖	↗	↗	↗	↗	↗	↗	

5-17a, b. Draft and band, Pattern 14.

Pattern 15

Warp Fiber: Four-ply Orlon
Filling Fiber: Same as warp (maroon)
Warp Ends: 44
Warp Breakdown: 22 White
                     11 Blue
                     11 Maroon
Turning: 16F / 16B

This is also a three-color vertical stripe (as is Pattern 14), but it looks quite different. The cards are all threaded in one direction; the turn reversals are marked by alternating long blue and white stitches. Notice how the slant of the stitches changes with each turn reversal.

11	10	9	8	7	6	5	4	3	2	1	
M	M	M	M	M	M	M	M	M	M	M	A
W	W	W	W	W	W	W	W	W	W	W	B
B	B	B	B	B	B	B	B	B	B	B	C
W	W	W	W	W	W	W	W	W	W	W	D
↖	↖	↖	↖	↖	↖	↖	↖	↖	↖	↖	

5-18a, b. Draft and band, Pattern 15.

Pattern 16

Warp Fiber: Four-ply crochet cotton
Filling Fiber: Two-ply crochet cotton (pink)
Warp Ends: 116
Warp Breakdown: 29 Pink
                       29 Yellow
                       29 Blue
                       29 Green

Turning: 4F / 4B

This stripe, shown in Color Plate C-9, is very bright and gay. It adds a festive touch to almost any outfit.

Pattern 17

Warp Fiber: Lightweight rattail and three-line braid
Filling Fiber: Three-line braid
Warp Ends: 120
Warp Breakdown: 60 Navy blue, line braid
                       60 Navy blue, rattail

Turning: 8F / 8B

Using two different fibers in the same shade of navy blue results in *textured stripes*, rather than colored stripes.

5-19. Draft for Pattern 16.

25	24	23	22	21	20	19	18	17	16	15	14	13	12	11	10	9	8	7	6	5	4	3	2	1	
B	B	B	B	B	B	B	B	B	B	B	B	B	B	B	B	B	B	B	B	B	B	B	B	B	A
Y	Y	Y	Y	Y	Y	Y	Y	Y	Y	Y	Y	Y	Y	Y	Y	Y	Y	Y	Y	Y	Y	Y	Y	Y	B
G	G	G	G	G	G	G	G	G	G	G	G	G	G	G	G	G	G	G	G	G	G	G	G	G	C
P	P	P	P	P	P	P	P	P	P	P	P	P	P	P	P	P	P	P	P	P	P	P	P	P	D
↘	↘	↘	↘	↘	↘	↘	↘	↘	↘	↘	↗	↗	↗	↗	↗	↗	↗	↗	↗	↗	↗	↗	↗	↗	

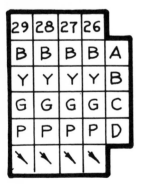

29	28	27	26	
B	B	B	B	A
Y	Y	Y	Y	B
G	G	G	G	C
P	P	P	P	D
↘	↘	↘	↘	

25	24	23	22	21	20	19	18	17	16	15	14	13	12	11	10	9	8	7	6	5	4	3	2	1	
L	L	L	L	L	L	L	L	L	L	L	L	L	L	L	L	L	L	L	L	L	L	L	L	L	A
R	R	R	R	R	R	R	R	R	R	R	R	R	R	R	R	R	R	R	R	R	R	R	R	R	B
L	L	L	L	L	L	L	L	L	L	L	L	L	L	L	L	L	L	L	L	L	L	L	L	L	C
R	R	R	R	R	R	R	R	R	R	R	R	R	R	R	R	R	R	R	R	R	R	R	R	R	D
↖	↖	↖	↖	↖	↖	↖	↖	↖	↖	↗	↗	↗	↗	↗	↗	↗	↗	↗	↗	↗	↗	↗	↗	↗	

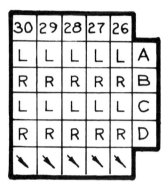

30	29	28	27	26	
L	L	L	L	L	A
R	R	R	R	R	B
L	L	L	L	L	C
R	R	R	R	R	D
↖	↖	↖	↖	↖	

5-20a, b. Draft and band, Pattern 17.

BOX DESIGNS

The following patterns are all relatively easy to thread and even easier to see on paper. Interesting variations can be made from the simple box design, which is a small motif against a solid ground. The box itself may be uni- or multi-colored; similarly, boxes of different colored solids can be planned for one band. The shape of the box unit may be square or rectangular, woven vertically or horizontally on the band.

In this chapter only simple box designs appear. There are more complicated applications of these principles which you may want to try as you become a more proficient weaver. You will want to incorporate the turn reversal into this motif to achieve new shapes on the band. Overall design can include many different boxes of varied shapes and colors.

The basic pattern draft for a box design appears in Figure 5-21 based on ten cards.

Key points to remember:

- Boxes appear to their best advantage when placed against a solid field.
- The pattern looks neatest when the box unit is threaded so that the stitches are symmetric.
- Shape and size of the box unit depends on: number of cards in the motif, number of holes of those cards bearing the box colors, and the turning sequence.

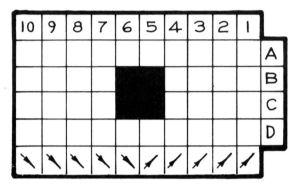

5-21. Model twenty-card draft for the box design.

Pattern 18

Warp Fiber: Soutache
Filling Fiber: Same as warp (Nile green)
Warp Ends: 40
Warp Breakdown: 28 Nile green
                          12 Peach
Turning: All Forward

Soutache is not a good fiber to use for the box design; it is much better for herringbones. Nonetheless, the box motif is visible here.

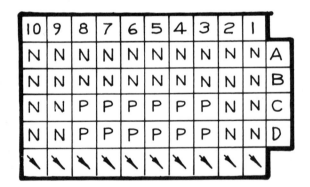

5-22a, b. Draft and band, Pattern 18.

56

Pattern 19

Warp Fiber: Heavy rattail
Filling Fiber: Light rattail (avocado)
Warp Ends: 40
Warp Breakdown: 24 Orange
                16 Avocado
Turning: All Forward

Notice that all four holes in cards 5 and 6 are threaded with the same color. That is the basic principle in the threading of horizontal stripes, so there will be one horizontal stripe down the length of the band, connecting the boxes.

10	9	8	7	6	5	4	3	2	1	
A	A	A	A	O	O	A	A	A	A	A
A	A	A	A	O	O	A	A	A	A	B
A	A	O	O	O	O	O	O	A	A	C
A	A	O	O	O	O	O	O	A	A	D
↘	↘	↘	↘	↘	↘	↘	↘	↘	↘	

5-23a, b. Draft and band, Pattern 19.

Pattern 20

Warp Fiber: Novelty thread (Christmas package tie)
Filling Fiber: Same as warp (gold)
Warp Ends: 72
Warp Breakdown: 36 Gold
                36 Silver
Turning: All Forward

This band is used as a strap for a black pocketbook in Color Plate C-10. The detail shown here, clearly shows how symmetric threading looks. For a box pattern such as this, the threading could be executed in groups of six (cards), each group being symmetric (the first three cards threaded B-to-F and the next three cards threaded F-to-B), instead of how the threading appears here (the first nine cards threaded B-to-F, and the next nine threaded F-to-B).

5-24a, b. Draft and band, Pattern 20.

18	17	16	15	14	13	12	11	10	9	8	7	6	5	4	3	2	1	
G	G	G	G	G	G	S	S	S	S	S	G	G	G	G	G	A
G	G	G	G	G	G	S	S	S	S	S	S	G	G	G	G	G	B
S	S	S	S	S	S	S	G	G	G	G	G	G	S	S	S	S	S	C
S	S	S	S	S	S	S	G	G	G	G	G	S	S	S	S	S	D
↘	↘	↘	↘	↘	↘	↘	↘	↘	↗	↗	↗	↗	↗	↗	↗	↗	↗	

Pattern 21

Warp Fiber: Chainnette
Filling Fiber: Same as warp (blue)
Warp Ends: 88
Warp Breakdown: 56 Blue
                 32 Yellow
Turning: All Forward

Compare the width of this band, shown in Color Plate C-14, to the preceding one. Pattern 23 has only 18 cards, yet it is twice the width of this one. The band from Pattern 22 is based on a draft very similar to this one, but is also twice as wide as this one. This should underscore the principle that it is not only the number of cards which determines the width of a band, but also the gauge of the fiber used.

5-25. Draft for Pattern 21.

22	21	20	19	18	17	16	15	14	13	12	11	10	9	8	7	6	5	4	3	2	1	
B	B	B	B	B	B	B	Y	Y	Y	Y	B	B	B	B	Y	Y	Y	Y	B	B	B	A
B	B	B	B	B	B	B	Y	Y	Y	Y	B	B	B	B	Y	Y	Y	Y	B	B	B	B
B	B	B	Y	Y	Y	Y	B	B	B	B	Y	Y	Y	Y	B	B	B	B	B	B	B	C
B	B	B	Y	Y	Y	Y	B	B	B	B	Y	Y	Y	Y	B	B	B	B	B	B	B	D

Pattern 22

Warp Fiber: Heavy rattail
Filling Fiber: Thin rattail (black)
Warp Ends: 104
Warp Breakdown: 64 Black
                 10 Pink
                 10 Gold
                 10 Light blue
                 10 Kelly green
Turning: All Forward

Compare the colors and texture of this band, shown in Color Plate C-9, to Pattern 23. Both are woven with the same colors, but the effects are very different.

Pattern 23

Warp Fiber: Chainnette
Filling Fiber: Same as warp (black)
Warp Ends: 136
Warp Breakdown: 104 Black
                 8 Yellow
                 8 Green
                 8 Light blue
                 8 Pink
Turning: All Forward

This band is shown in Color Plates C-9 and C-20. Compare it with Pattern 22.

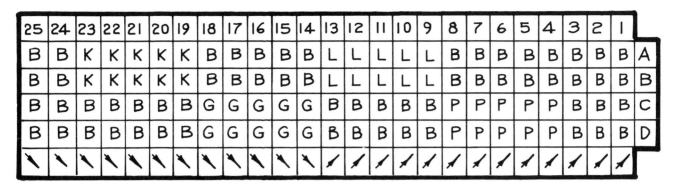

5-26. Draft for Pattern 22.

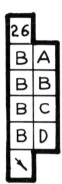

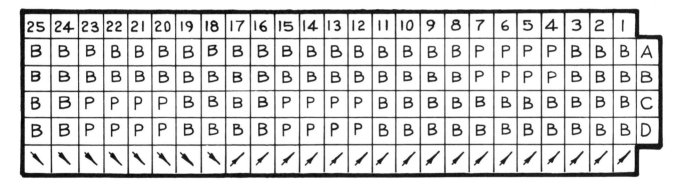

5-27. Draft for Pattern 23.

34	33	32	31	30	29	28	27	26	
B	B	B	G	G	G	G	B	B	A
B	B	B	G	G	G	G	B	B	B
B	B	B	B	B	B	B	B	B	C
B	B	B	B	B	B	B	B	B	D
↙	↙	↙	↙	↙	↙	↙	↙	↙	

DIAGONAL STRIPES

Once you can recognize vertical and horizontal stripes, you will have very little difficulty assimilating the pattern structure for diagonal stripes. With the former two types of stripes, a distinct pattern for each was developed. The box design motif was built on those two principles. The structure for the diagonal stripe goes one step further. See if you can determine the basic framework for diagonal stripes while looking at the following patterns. First study the basic pattern draft, presented below. Notice the checkerboard effect, which is the building block of all diagonal stripes. Try to connect the shaded boxes with oblique lines, so that 1B is connected to 2A and 1D is connected with 2C, 3B, 4A, and so on. This is one direction in which the diagonal line can flow. Erase those pencil lines and now connect 5D, 4C, 3B, 2A, as well as 3D, 2C, 1B, and you will see that the diagonal line moves in the opposite direction.* Regardless of how you follow the diagonal lines made by the alternating blocks of color, you will get a diagonal stripe.

A basic diagonal pattern is quite versatile, as you will discover in the successive exercises. The way in which the stripes result is a function of both the turning and threading directions.

*In both these cases, and in the successive experiments, the description of the movement of the diagonal line will be described in terms of upward motion, since that is how the weaving proceeds. That is to say, a line that slants up to the right could also be described as slanting down to the left. In this volume all diagonal lines are described in terms of "up."

To understand how diagonal lines unfurl as you weave them, try this short experiment. Make another pattern exactly identical to Figure 5-28 omitting the bottom row intended for threading directions. Place your drawing directly on top of the draft in the book, covering the numbers of the cards presented along the top edge of the draft. The bottom edge of your draft should be flush against the top edge of the book draft. Again, trace the possible movement of the stripes with your eye and you will discover that the stripes build in such a manner so that the second set of four turns (your draft) extends those stripes that have already been woven with by the first set of four turns (the draft in the book). This weaving process is discussed in greater detail in Chapter 9.

Key points to remember:

- To obtain a smooth diagonal line, the slant of the stitch *must* be the same as the angle of the diagonal line.
- Key variables in any diagonal pattern are the threading directions and the turning method.
- To achieve a stitch that slants to the upper left, either:
  a. thread the card B-to-F and weave Forward, or
  b. thread the card F-to-B and weave Backward.
- To achieve a stitch that slants to the upper right, either:
  a. thread the card F-to-B and weave Forward, or
  b. thread the card B-to-F and weave Backward.
- The slant of the diagonal line changes when the turning direction changes.

5-28. Model twenty-card draft for diagonal stripes.

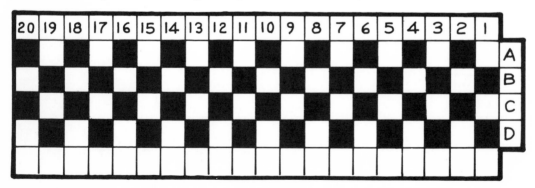

Pattern 24

Warp Fiber: Rug yarn
Filling Fiber: Same as warp (pink)
Warp Ends: 44
Warp Breakdown: 22 Pink
                 22 Green
Turning: All Forward

   Both sides of this band produce clearly defined diagonal stripes.

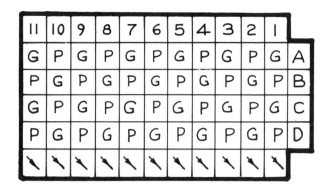

11	10	9	8	7	6	5	4	3	2	1	
G	P	G	P	G	P	G	P	G	P	G	A
P	G	P	G	P	G	P	G	P	G	P	B
G	P	G	P	G	P	G	P	G	P	G	C
P	G	P	G	P	G	P	G	P	G	P	D
↘	↘	↘	↘	↘	↘	↘	↘	↘	↘	↘	

5-29a, b. Draft and band, Pattern 24.

Pattern 25

Warp Fiber: Thin rattail
Filling Fiber: Same as warp (gold)
Warp Ends: 40
Warp Breakdown: 20 Gold
                 20 Maroon
Turning: 12F / 12B

   The angle of the diagonal produced by the first 12 Forward turns of this pattern (threaded B-to-F) is opposite to the angle produced by the first 12 Forward turns of Pattern 24 (threaded F-to-B). What is basically the same pattern results in different slants when threaded in different directions. The angle of the diagonal changes in this pattern when the turning direction changes. In the 12B series of turns, the diagonal resembles that in Pattern 24. Remember these examples when you weave the Diagonal Experiment on page 65.

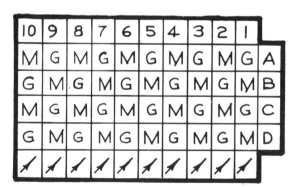

10	9	8	7	6	5	4	3	2	1	
M	G	M	G	M	G	M	G	M	A
G	M	G	M	G	M	G	M	G	B
M	G	M	G	M	G	M	G	M	C
G	M	G	M	G	M	G	M	G	D
↙	↙	↙	↙	↙	↙	↙	↙	↙	

5-30a, b. Draft and band, Pattern 25.

Pattern 26
Warp Fiber: Chainnette
Filling Fiber: Same as warp (peach)
Warp Ends: 120
Warp Breakdown: 60 Yellow
                      60 Peach
Turning: 24F / 24B

This pattern results in a very clean, neat diagonal of double-stitch width. Again, as in Pattern 25, the angle of the diagonal changes when the direction of the turning changes.

Pattern 27
Warp Fiber: "Wintuk," two-ply Orlon
Filling Fiber: Same as warp (red)
Warp Ends: 100
Warp Breakdown: 50 Red
                      25 Blue
                      25 Green
Turning: 8F / 8B

This diagonal pattern makes an interesting wave at the point of turn reversal. Because of the three colors used, the design seems more complicated than it really is. This is a fine example of how color affects the patterning in card weaving.

5-31a, b. Draft and band, Pattern 26.

25	24	23	22	21	20	19	18	17	16	15	14	13	12	11	10	9	8	7	6	5	4	3	2	1	
Y	Y	P	P	Y	Y	P	P	Y	Y	P	P	Y	Y	P	P	Y	Y	P	P	Y	Y	P	P	Y	A
P	Y	Y	P	P	Y	Y	P	P	Y	Y	P	P	Y	Y	P	P	Y	Y	P	P	Y	Y	P	P	B
P	P	Y	Y	P	P	Y	Y	P	P	Y	Y	P	P	Y	Y	P	P	Y	Y	P	P	Y	Y	P	C
Y	P	P	Y	Y	P	P	Y	Y	P	P	Y	Y	P	P	Y	Y	P	P	Y	Y	P	P	Y	Y	D
✓	✓	✓	✓	✓	✓	✓	✓	✓	✓	✓	✓	✓	✓	✓	✓	✓	✓	✓	✓	✓	✓	✓	✓	✓	

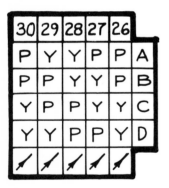

30	29	28	27	26	
P	Y	Y	P	P	A
P	P	Y	Y	P	B
Y	P	P	Y	Y	C
Y	Y	P	P	Y	D
✓	✓	✓	✓	✓	

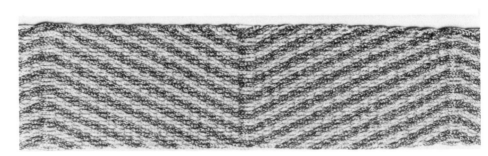

25	24	23	22	21	20	19	18	17	16	15	14	13	12	11	10	9	8	7	6	5	4	3	2	1	
R	G	R	B	R	G	R	B	R	G	R	B	R	G	R	B	R	G	R	B	R	G	R	B	R	A
B	R	G	R	B	R	G	R	B	R	G	R	B	R	G	R	B	R	G	R	B	R	G	R	B	B
R	B	R	G	R	B	R	G	R	B	R	G	R	B	R	G	R	B	R	G	R	B	R	G	R	C
G	R	B	R	G	R	B	R	G	R	B	R	G	R	B	R	G	R	B	R	G	R	B	R	G	D
↙	↙	↙	↙	↙	↙	↙	↙	↙	↙	↙	↙	↙	↙	↙	↙	↙	↙	↙	↙	↙	↙	↙	↙	↙	

5-32a, b. Draft and band, Pattern 27.

Pattern 28
Warp Fiber: Heavy rattail
Filling Fiber: Thin two-ply cotton (pink)
Warp Ends: 40
Warp Breakdown: 14 Blue
　　　　　　　　 13 Pink
　　　　　　　　 13 Green
Turning: 12F / 12B

The "neat" side of this diagonal, as shown in Color Plate C-15, results on the bottom of the band, as it is woven. This is because the threading is F-to-B.

10	9	8	7	6	5	4	3	2	1	
B	G	P	B	G	P	B	G	P	B	A
P	B	G	P	B	G	P	B	G	P	B
G	P	B	G	P	B	G	P	B	G	C
B	G	P	B	G	P	B	G	P	B	D
↘	↘	↘	↘	↘	↘	↘	↘	↘	↘	

5-33. Draft for Pattern 28.

Pattern 29

Warp Fiber: Perlé (90% acrylic and 10% vinyon)
Filling Fiber: Same as warp (lilac)
Warp Ends: 88
Warp Breakdown: 22 Lilac
22 Pink
22 Green
22 Yellow

Turning: 16F / 16B

This pattern, as is Pattern 28, is threaded F-to-B and results in a band with the "neat" side on the bottom as it is woven. It is illustrated in Color Plate C-11.

It should now be apparent what a pattern for a diagonal stripe looks like when drafted. The diagonal itself is very obvious as a "step" pattern in the draft. The following exercise will help you understand the basic principles involved and provide a handy reference for future use.

Two basic drafts are used to achieve diagonals, as shown in Figures 5-35 and 5-36, labelled Diagonal Pattern A and Diagonal Pattern B. Notice that the stripes in Pattern A are angled in the opposite direction of those in Pattern B. For maximum clarity, the diagonal is presented as a single dark line on a light field. These stripes are different from those in 5-28, where every card had two light colors and two dark colors. In this pattern, only one warp end per card bears the color for the stripe—the result is a thin stripe against a contrasting color, as background (or you may even view the second color as a wide stripe). It is important to also note that you cannot connect the shaded boxes of Pattern A in either direction, as you did with those in Figure 5-28. You can connect them only in one direction—and the resulting diagonal slants up to the right. Similarly, the colored boxes in Pattern B can be connected in only one fashion—resulting in stripes that slant up to the left. Because of this, only one side of the band will bear a well-defined

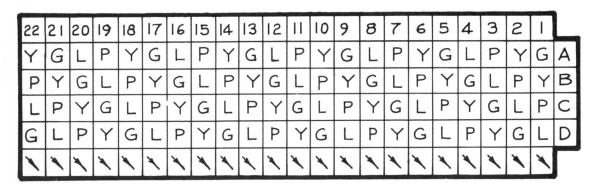

5-34. Draft for Pattern 29.

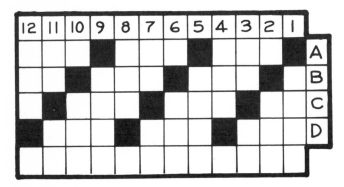

5-35. Diagonal Pattern A.

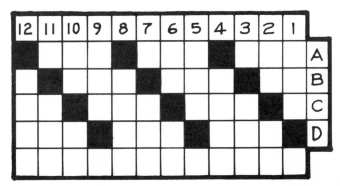

5-36. Diagonal Pattern B.

diagonal line. It is for this reason that Patterns 24 and 25 result in neat diagonals on both sides of the bands and Patterns 26, 27, 28, and 29 have a smooth diagonal on only one side.

As previously noted, most diagonal patterns have a "neat," defined side, and a "feathery," unaligned side. This is because it is the smoothness of the unbroken diagonal line in the pattern that gives it definition when woven. This smoothness results from the slant of the stitches. Because of the principles of threading and turning, only one side can have that smoothness, particularly in diagonal patterns such as these two.

Bearing this in mind throughout the following discussion, the neat, aligned side is referred to as the *even* side, and the unaligned side is referred to as the *uneven* side. The terms *top* and *bottom* connote the sides of the band as they result while the weaving is performed.

Diagonal Pattern A and Diagonal Pattern B (Figures 5-35 and 5-36) are the mainstays of the following experiment summarized in Figure 5-37. The best way to execute this experiment is to weave the eight variations in numerical order. To do so you will have to construct four separate looms.

Variation 1
    Pattern A
    Threaded B-to-F
    Turning: All Forward

Variation 2
    Pattern A
    Threaded B-to-F
    Turning: All Backward

Variation 3
    Pattern A
    Threaded F-to-B
    Turning: All Forward

Variation 4
    Pattern A
    Threaded F-to-B
    Turning: All Backward

Variation 5
    Pattern B
    Threaded B-to-F
    Turning: All Forward

Variation 6
    Pattern B
    Threaded B-to-F
    Turning: All Backward

Variation 7
    Pattern B
    Threaded F-to-B
    Turning: All Forward

Variation 8
    Pattern B
    Threaded F-to-B
    Turning: All Backward

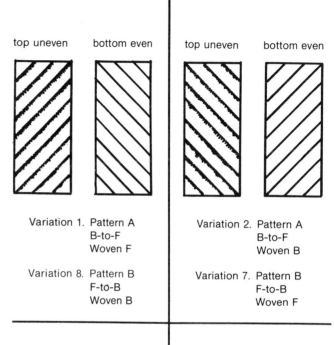

top uneven   bottom even   top uneven   bottom even

Variation 1. Pattern A
    B-to-F
    Woven F

Variation 8. Pattern B
    F-to-B
    Woven B

Variation 2. Pattern A
    B-to-F
    Woven B

Variation 7. Pattern B
    F-to-B
    Woven F

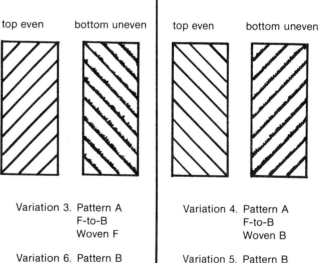

top even   bottom uneven   top even   bottom uneven

Variation 3. Pattern A
    F-to-B
    Woven F

Variation 6. Pattern B
    B-to-F
    Woven B

Variation 4. Pattern A
    F-to-B
    Woven B

Variation 5. Pattern B
    B-to-F
    Woven F

5-37. This chart summarizes the results of the diagonal experiment, for handy reference.

Weave at least a few inches of each variation. Mark the beginning and ending of each. Label the sample with the variation number, specific directions, etc. Be certain that you followed the prescribed directions for each. When you have finished all eight variations, it will be apparent that there are several ways to achieve the same result.

The variables are:
1. the direction (slant) of the diagonal angle in the pattern
2. the threading direction
3. the turning direction

It should be clear from the summary presented in Figure 5-37, that you can achieve the same result (that is, with a specific, given diagonal pattern) by threading F-to-B and weaving Backward as by threading B-to-F and weaving Forward. The one difference is that on one band the "neat" side is on the top of the weaving and on the other band it is on the bottom. Generally, that does not matter, for when the band comes off the loom, either side could be used as the "show" side.

When you are planning a particular design, however, that requires the use of diagonal lines (as part of a pattern, area of color, or outline, and not necessarily as a stripe motif), think before you start to draft. In which direction do you want the line to move? If it is to the upper left, then check the chart and see which combinations will give that result. They are Variations 4 and 5. Since it is likely that either all, or at least the first half of the design will be woven forward, then you must select Diagonal Pattern B, threaded B-to-F, and woven Forward. If you look back to Diagonal Pattern B, you will of course find that the diagonal lines of Pattern B move to the upper left. This is far from a coincidence—it is a very important building block of card weaving and helps determine how a pattern will translate to the woven form.

The slant of the stitches plays a role here and in every other pattern (see Figure 5-38a, b, and c). The stitches on the top side of a band slant in the opposite direction from those on the bottom. This is always true. It is for this reason that: (1) a diagonal pattern such as in Figure 5-27 results in "neat" diagonal lines on both sides of the band because the diagonal lines (the shaded boxes you connected) can be joined in either direction; and (2)

the two types of turn reversal (discussed in Chapter 4) differ from the top of the band to the bottom.

Whenever in doubt about designing a new pattern or changing an existing one, refer to Figure 5-37, so that you can anticipate how the desired effects can be achieved in the woven form.

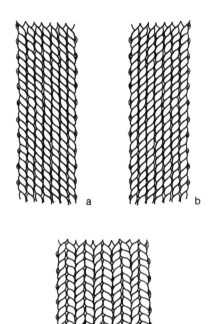

5-38. The variations in stitching which emerged in the Diagonal Experiment comprise one of the foundation blocks of card weaving. Learn to recognize the slant of a stitch and know what it means.
a. The direction of these stitches is upward to the left; this look is achieved by either threading a card B-to-F and weaving F, or threading F-to-B and weaving B.
b. The direction of these stitches is upward to the right; this look is achieved by either threading a card F-to-B and weaving F, or B-to-F and weaving B.
c. The "knitted" look of this band is the result of threading adjacent cards in opposite directions. Can you determine the two possible ways this look might be achieved?

CHEVRONS/HERRINGBONES

Once you can detect the diagonal lines in the preceding section, you will have no trouble with the following patterns—they are all varieties of chevrons or herringbones. A sample pattern draft is given in Figure 5-39. This draft is for a sixteen-card loom, with a two-color pattern. The heavy black line represents the point at which the threading direction changes and the pattern "flips over." This results in symmetry which creates a central core from which diagonals emanate to form the herringbone or chevron. Note the similarity of each half of this pattern to Diagonal Patterns A and B in the preceding section.

This structure is the basis for all the following patterns. Glance at them and see if you can find the central core(s) in each.

Similarly, Figure 5-40 is another draft, representative of the basic type used to produce chevrons. Unlike Figure 5-39, however, the chevron lines are the width of two boxes on the grid, not one. In both Figures 5-39 and 5-40 threading directions are presented which help to delineate the central core from which the chevron pattern radiates.

Diagonals such as these were the mainstays of early Egyptian patterns. (See Figures 2-1, 2-18, and 6-23)

Key points to remember:
- The slants of the diagonals composing the herringbones and chevrons must be planned quite carefully, using the principles learned in the Diagonal Experiment.
- For a well-defined chevron the two oppositely slanted diagonals must meet head on.

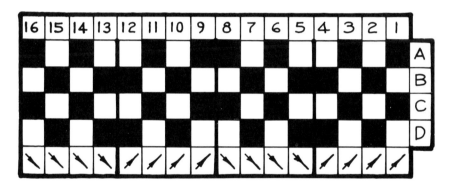

5-39. Model sixteen-card draft for chevrons and herringbones.

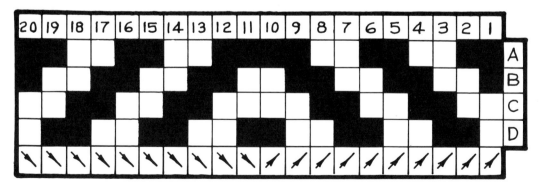

5-40. A twenty-card draft for the basic two-stitch-wide chevron pattern, with threading directions.

25	24	23	22	21	20	19	18	17	16	15	14	13	12	11	10	9	8	7	6	5	4	3	2	1	
C	C	B	B	C	C	B	T	T	T	T	B	C	C	B	B	C	C	B	B	C	T	T	T	T	A
C	B	B	C	C	B	B	T	T	T	T	B	B	C	C	B	B	C	C	B	B	T	T	T	T	B
B	B	C	C	B	B	C	T	T	T	T	C	B	B	C	C	B	B	C	C	B	T	T	T	T	C
B	C	C	B	B	C	C	T	T	T	T	C	C	B	B	C	C	B	B	C	C	T	T	T	T	D
↙	↙	↙	↙	↙	↙	↙	↙	↙	↗	↗	↗	↗	↗	↗	↗	↗	↗	↗	↗	↗	↗	↗	↗	↗	

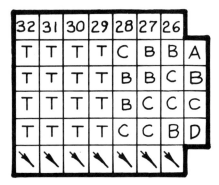

32	31	30	29	28	27	26	
T	T	T	T	C	B	B	A
T	T	T	T	B	B	C	B
T	T	T	T	B	C	C	C
T	T	T	T	C	C	B	D
↙	↙	↙	↙	↙	↙	↙	

5-41a, b. Draft and band, Pattern 30.

Pattern 30

Warp Fiber: Perlé
Filling Fiber: Same as warp (turquoise)
Warp Ends: 128
Warp Breakdown: 48 Turquoise
　　　　　　　　40 Brown
　　　　　　　　40 Cream
Turning: All Forward

This pattern is based on the basic two-stitch-wide draft in Figure 5-40, and is a combination of several different types of stripes: The borders are horizontal stripes as is the central core. The chevron effect is a result of the two angles of stripes, discussed previously, meeting at the central core.

Pattern 31

Warp Fiber: 100% Orlon
Filling Fiber: Same as warp (deep rose)
Warp Ends: 96
Warp Breakdown: 48 Rose, deep
                              48 Pink, light
Turning: All Forward

Compare this herringbone to Pattern 32, which is woven with the same colors. Note the very subtle difference between the two: This pattern renders a very neat herringbone, while Pattern 32 is not nearly so well aligned. Now compare Cards 3 and 4 in the drafts for Patterns 31 and 32. In Pattern 31 the two stitches forming the points of the herringbone are always the same color. In Pattern 32, these two stitches are always two different colors. Therefore, in order to achieve a well-defined arrowhead, the diagonal lines forming the arrowhead must meet head on.

24	23	22	21	20	19	18	17	16	15	14	13	12	11	10	9	8	7	6	5	4	3	2	1	
R	P	R	R	P	R	P	R	R	P	R	R	P	R	R	P	R	R	P	R	R	P	R	R	A
P	R	P	P	R	P	P	R	P	P	R	P	P	R	P	P	R	P	P	R	P	P	R	P	B
R	P	R	R	P	R	R	P	R	R	P	R	R	P	R	R	P	R	R	P	R	R	P	R	C
P	R	P	P	R	P	P	R	P	P	R	P	P	R	P	P	R	P	P	R	P	P	R	P	D
↙	↘	↙	↗	↗	↗	↘	↘	↘	↘	↗	↗	↗	↘	↘	↘	↗	↗	↗	↘	↘	↗	↗	↗	

5-42a, b. Draft and band, Pattern 31.

Pattern 32

Warp Fiber: 100% Orlon
Filling Fiber: Same as warp (deep rose)
Warp Ends: 96
Warp Breakdown: 48 Rose, deep
48 Pink, light
Turning: All Forward

After comparing this draft to Pattern draft 31, also look at Pattern drafts 24, 25, and 37. The drafts are all similar; the main difference is the *direction* in which the warp ends are threaded. Five very dissimilar designs surface from the same draft, threaded in different directions.

Pattern 33

Warp Fiber: Chainnette
Filling Fiber: Same as warp
Warp Ends: 80
Warp Breakdown: 40 Purple
40 Lilac
Turning: All Forward

Observe the similarities of this band to Pattern 26. The design in Pattern 26, however, repeats itself; here the design is "flipped over" at Card 6. At that point the direction of the threading is then changed and a new design results instead of a diagonal. Likewise, this pattern is similar to Pattern 30. Note the difference in the two drafts which make each pattern unique. This pattern is illustrated in Color Plate C-14.

24	23	22	21	20	19	18	17	16	15	14	13	12	11	10	9	8	7	6	5	4	3	2	1	
P	R	P	R	P	R	P	R	P	R	P	R	P	R	P	R	P	R	P	R	P	R	P	R	A
R	P	R	P	R	P	R	P	R	P	R	P	R	P	R	P	R	P	R	P	R	P	R	P	B
P	R	P	R	P	R	P	R	P	R	P	R	P	R	P	R	P	R	P	R	P	R	P	R	C
R	P	R	P	R	P	R	P	R	P	R	P	R	P	R	P	R	P	R	P	R	P	R	P	D

5-43a, b. Draft and band, Pattern 32.

70

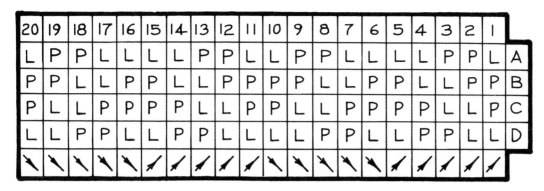

20	19	18	17	16	15	14	13	12	11	10	9	8	7	6	5	4	3	2	1	
L	P	P	L	L	L	L	P	P	L	L	P	P	L	L	L	L	P	P	L	A
P	P	L	L	P	P	L	L	P	P	P	P	L	L	P	P	L	L	P	P	B
P	L	L	P	P	P	P	L	L	P	P	L	L	P	P	P	P	L	L	P	C
L	L	P	P	L	L	P	P	L	L	L	L	P	P	L	L	P	P	L	L	D
↘	↘	↘	↘	↘	↘	↗	↗	↗	↗	↗	↘	↘	↘	↘	↘	↗	↗	↗	↗	

5-44. Draft for Pattern 33.

Pattern 34

Warp Fiber: Two-ply mercerized cotton
Filling Fiber: Same as warp (blue)
Warp Ends: 96
Warp Breakdown: 48 Blue
48 Yellow
Turning: All Forward

This charming band is a most unusual herringbone pattern. Notice that the entire B row on the draft is yellow. Naturally, you would expect that row to result in a vertical stripe; but in this case, a neat stripe does not result because the cards are not all threaded in the same direction.

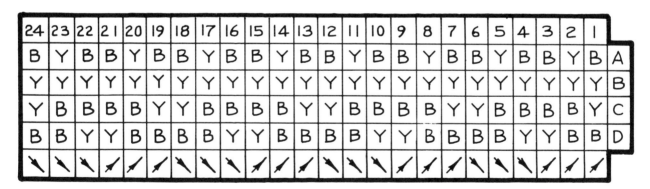

24	23	22	21	20	19	18	17	16	15	14	13	12	11	10	9	8	7	6	5	4	3	2	1	
B	Y	B	B	Y	B	B	Y	B	B	Y	B	B	Y	B	B	Y	B	B	Y	B	B	Y	B	A
Y	Y	Y	Y	Y	Y	Y	Y	Y	Y	Y	Y	Y	Y	Y	Y	Y	Y	Y	Y	Y	Y	Y	Y	B
Y	B	B	B	B	Y	Y	B	B	B	B	Y	Y	B	B	B	B	Y	Y	B	B	B	B	Y	C
B	B	Y	Y	B	B	B	B	Y	Y	B	B	B	B	Y	Y	B	B	B	B	Y	Y	B	B	D
↘	↘	↘	↘	↗	↗	↗	↗	↘	↘	↘	↘	↗	↗	↗	↗	↘	↘	↘	↘	↗	↗	↗	↗	

5-45a, b. Draft and band, Pattern 34.

Pattern 35

Warp Fiber: Heavy knitting wool
Filling Fiber: Lightweight Orlon (brown)
Warp Ends: 96
Warp Breakdown: 48 Rust
  48 Brown
Turning: All Forward

Although both Patterns 34 and 35 are woven with 24 cards, this band is twice as wide as Pattern 34 because of the heavy-gauge wool used. A third color could be used for the little crow's feet accent which are achieved by the warp ends in Hole D, Cards 4 and 5. Likewise, this pattern could be changed to a regular diagonal by transposing the colors of the warp ends in the A holes of Cards 4 and 5 with those in the D holes of the same cards.

Pattern 36

Warp Fiber: Thin rattail
Filling Fiber: Same as warp (copper)
Warp Ends: 40
Warp Breakdown: 20 Copper
  20 Peach
Turning: All Forward

You will note that the draft of this pattern follows the format of a vertical stripe. If all the cards of this pattern were threaded in the same direction, the resulting weave would be merely vertical stripes. Since they are threaded in symmetrical pairs, the band appears to be a very loosely defined herringbone-type stripe.

24	23	22	21	20	19	18	17	16	15	14	13	12	11	10	9	8	7	6	5	4	3	2	1	
R	B	B	B	B	B	B	R	R	B	B	B	B	B	B	R	R	B	B	B	B	B	R	A
B	B	R	R	R	B	B	B	B	R	R	R	B	B	B	B	R	R	R	R	B	B	B	B
B	R	R	B	B	R	R	B	B	R	R	B	B	R	R	B	B	R	R	B	B	R	R	B	C
R	R	B	R	R	B	R	R	R	B	R	R	B	R	R	R	B	R	R	B	R	R	D
↖	↖	↖	↖	↖	↗	↗	↗	↖	↖	↖	↖	↖	↖	↗	↗	↗	↗	↖	↖	↖	↗	↗	↗	

5-46a, b, and c. Draft and front and back of band, Pattern 35.

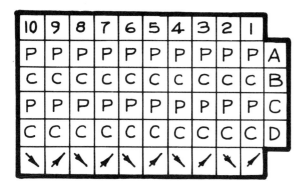

10	9	8	7	6	5	4	3	2	1	
P	P	P	P	P	P	P	P	P	P	A
C	C	C	C	C	C	C	C	C	C	B
P	P	P	P	P	P	P	P	P	P	C
C	C	C	C	C	C	C	C	C	C	D
↙	↗	↙	↗	↙	↗	↙	↗	↙	↗	

5-47a, b. Draft and band, Pattern 36.

Pattern 37

Warp Fiber: Thin rattail
Filling Fiber: Same as warp (white)
Warp Ends: 48
Warp Breakdown: 24 Black
                     24 White
Turning: All Forward

It has already been mentioned that this pattern is basically the same as Patterns 24 and 25 (and by extension, Patterns 31 and 32); because of threading, however, the result is startlingly different. This is, perhaps, my favorite pattern of the simple weaves.

12	11	10	9	8	7	6	5	4	3	2	1	
W	B	W	B	W	B	W	B	W	B	W	B	A
B	W	B	W	B	W	B	W	B	W	B	W	B
W	B	W	B	W	B	W	B	W	B	W	B	C
B	W	B	W	B	W	B	W	B	W	B	W	D
↙	↗	↙	↗	↙	↗	↙	↗	↙	↗	↙	↗	

5-48a, b. Draft and band, Pattern 37.

73

6. Turning Experiments

As discussed earlier, one draft can result in different designs when woven (that is, when the cards are turned) in different sequences and threaded in different arrangements. This principle was underscored with Pattern 37. Taking this tenet one step further, you can use pattern drafts already presented, turn the cards in unusual sequences, and get very stylized bands which will be different from those already achieved.

COMBINING DIFFERENT TURNING SEQUENCES
Pattern 38
Warp Fiber: Chainnette
Filling Fiber: Same as warp
Warp Ends: 120
Warp Breakdown: 60 Dark brown
                         60 Yellow
Turning: 8F / 8B / 12F / 12B / repeat

Combining turning cycles of different lengths (8 and 12) results in a pattern with constant variety.

25	24	23	22	21	20	19	18	17	16	15	14	13	12	11	10	9	8	7	6	5	4	3	2	1	
D	D	Y	Y	D	D	Y	Y	D	D	D	D	Y	Y	D	D	Y	Y	D	D	D	D	Y	Y	D	A
Y	D	D	Y	Y	Y	Y	D	D	Y	Y	D	D	Y	Y	Y	Y	D	D	Y	Y	D	D	Y	Y	B
Y	Y	D	D	Y	Y	D	D	D	Y	Y	Y	Y	D	D	Y	Y	D	D	Y	Y	Y	Y	D	D	C
D	Y	Y	D	D	D	D	Y	Y	D	D	Y	Y	D	D	D	D	Y	Y	D	D	Y	Y	D	D	D
↗	↗	↗	↗	↗	↗	↖	↖	↖	↖	↖	↗	↗	↗	↗	↗	↖	↖	↖	↖	↖	↗	↗	↗	↗	

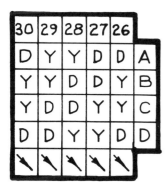

30	29	28	27	26	
D	Y	Y	D	D	A
Y	Y	D	D	Y	B
Y	D	D	Y	Y	C
D	D	Y	Y	D	D
↖	↖	↖	↖	↖	

6-1a, b, c. Draft and front and back sides of band, Pattern 38.

Pattern 39A

Warp Fiber: 6/3 twist (a fiber used in the millinery trade)
Filling Fiber: Same as warp (blue)
Warp Ends: 80
Warp Breakdown: 40 Blue (X)
40 Bright green (0)
Turning:
First: 2B / 1F / 3B / 1F / 4B / 1F / 3B /
1F / 2B / 1F / repeat once.
Then: 2F / 1B / 3F / 1B / 4F / 1B / 3F /
1B / 2F / 1B / repeat once.
Return to first turning sequence and repeat.

This draft is similar to Patterns 26, 30, and 33. Because of the turning directions, however; the bands are quite different. Moreover, this is the exact draft of Pattern 39B, but it is almost impossible to believe from the patterns derived. Now compare the turning directions to those for Pattern 39B.

TURNING CARDS IN GROUPS (PACKETS)
Pattern 39B

Warp Fiber: Four-ply wool
Filling Fiber: Same as warp (yellow)
Warp Ends: 80
Warp Breakdown: 40 Blue (X)
40 Yellow (O)
Turning:

Cards 1-10	Cards 11-20
4F / 4B	4B / 4F
4F / 4B	4B / 4F
8F / 8B	8B / 8F
Repeat	Repeat

This pattern is based on the draft for Pattern 36A with different turning directions. To execute the turning, divide the cards into two groups, putting cards 1-10 in one group (referred to as Packet 1) and cards 11-20 in another group (referred to as Packet 2). Advance Packet 1 along the warp, away from your body. Before turning any of the cards,

20	19	18	17	16	15	14	13	12	11	10	9	8	7	6	5	4	3	2	1	
O	O	X	X	O	O	X	X	O	O	X	X	O	O	X	X	O	O	X	X	A
X	O	O	X	X	O	O	X	X	O	O	X	X	O	O	X	X	O	O	X	B
X	X	O	O	X	X	O	O	X	X	O	O	X	X	O	O	X	X	O	O	C
O	X	X	O	O	X	X	O	O	X	X	O	O	X	X	O	O	X	X	O	D
↗	↗	↗	↗	↗	↗	↗	↗	↗	↗	↗	↗	↗	↗	↗	↗	↗	↗	↗	↗	

6-2. Draft for patterns 39A and 39B.

6 3. Pattern 39A.

76

feed the filling through the shed as you normally would. Then, turn each packet once in the indicated direction. Clean the shed, put the filling through and proceed to the next turn—again 1F for Cards 1–10, and 1B for Cards 11–20. After four turns, change the positions of the packets along the warp so that Packet 1 is closer to you than Packet 2.

It is always a good idea, when weaving patterns in which the cards have been divided into packets, to keep those packets turning Forward *ahead* (along the warp) and those packets turning Backward back along the warp, closer to your body. In that way, you always know that the forward packets get turned Forward and the back packets get turned Backward.

Likewise, by keeping the cards separated into packets, you avoid the common error of turning border cards in the wrong direction. Border cards indicates those cards which separate the packets— in this case Cards 10 and 11—not the cards along the outside edges, or Cards 1 and 20. There may

be a time when you are weaving with over fifty cards, divided into six or more packets. It is, therefore, a good idea to establish rules for yourself that make the weaving easy and prevent you from making careless errors.

After completing this experiment, return to the original draft and compare it to Diagonal Pattern B. It is, of course, very similar, except that the diagonals are two cards wide. Bearing this likeness in mind, consult the Diagonal Experiment Chart in Figure 5-37 while reconstructing the band mentally, following the directions presented for this experiment. You will most likely discover that you could have easily foretold what this band would look like by drawing on the principles outlined in that chart.

6-4a, b. Front and back sides of band, Pattern 39B.

CHANGING THE HOME POSITION

This exercise illustrates how different patterns may be achieved by changing not only the turning sequences, but also the Home Position. Each of the following bands was derived from the same draft, which is also the draft for Pattern 33 using only twenty cards.

Nearly every pattern for card weaving is written for the standard A–D Home Position—never assume otherwise unless specifically told so. It is, however, possible to change Home Positions when experimenting with or drafting new designs, as shown below. In cases such as these, get into the habit of noting your place to avoid confusion—and, moreover, to be able to reproduce any experiment that is successful.

Each turn made without filling to change the Home Position will cause the warp to twist at the far end, as any turn always does. Remember that these twists at the far end of the warp will always be there, even after weaving Backward to return to the new Home Position. Therefore, it is impossible to distinguish the Home Position by looking for a clean shed at the far end of the loom (which is normally a signal to the weaver that a commensurate amount of Forward and Backward turns have been woven, taking out the twists).

If, however, you depend on a clean shed at the far end to indicate that you have returned to Home Position, or to determine your position in a pattern, then by all means, arrange the loom so that the new Home Position is truly a Home Position, free of tangles at the far end. Do this after the loom is constructed and the cards have been turned to the desired new position. Release the loom from the doorknob (or whatever is holding the far end stationary), untie the warp ends, untangle the ends by combing them with your fingers, and retie them, and finally resecure the loom to the doorknob. This is a lot of trouble, but if it helps keep your mind free of confusion, then it is well worth it.

Patterns 40A–G
Warp Fiber: Cordé
Filling Fiber: Same as warp (black and white)
Warp Ends: 120
Warp Breakdown: 60 Black
                60 White

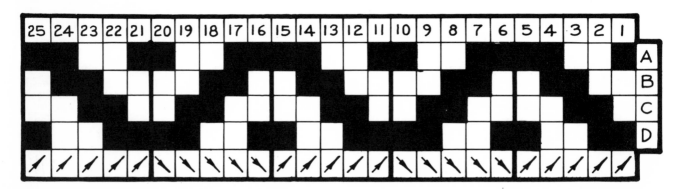

6-5. Draft for Patterns 40A–G. The shaded and blank areas, show the basic pattern; the "print-outs" of this pattern will vary with the different experimental turning sequences.

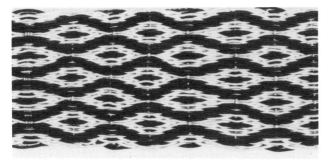

6-6a, b. Front and back of band, Pattern 40A.

Pattern 40A
Turning: 4F / 4B

This is a regular weave using no special techniques; diamond shapes are the result. The dark black center in the middle of the white oval results from the 2 black warp ends in the D holes in Cards 5 and 6, 15 and 16, 25 and 26, as well as the A holes in Cards 10 and 11, and 20 and 21. The black centers are all long stitches, representing the turn reversal.

Pattern 40B
Turning: 8F / 8B

Notice how herringbones start to appear in between each set of diamonds. This is a result of the expanded forward turning.

Pattern 40C
Turning: 12F / 12B

Now herringbones appear regularly and the diamond shapes appear only at the points of the turn reversals.

6-7a, b. Front and back of band, Pattern 40B.

6-8a, b. Front and back of band, Pattern 40C.

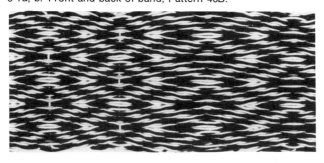

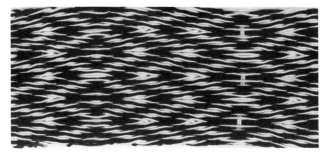

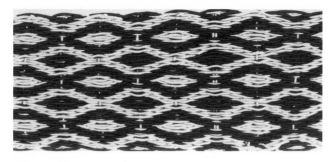

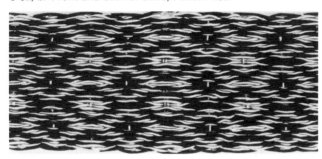

6-9a, b. Front and back of band, Pattern 40D.

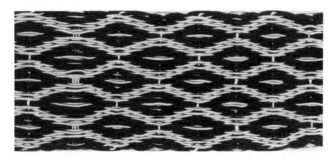

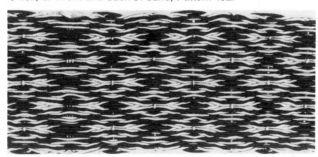

6-10a, b. Front and back of band, Pattern 40E.

Pattern 40D

Turning: 4F / 4B Woven with new Home Position of D–C

To change the standard Home Position from A–D to D–C (D furthest from you, C closest to you), simply turn the cards 1 turn Forward (without filling), and start weaving from there, in the new Home Position.

Pattern 40E

Turning: 4F / 4B Woven with new Home Position of C–B

To reach this Home Position from the normal A–D Home Position, simply turn the cards two turns Forward without filling. Start weaving from that point. Notice that this design has reverse coloration from Figure 6-6a.

Pattern 40F

Turning: 4F / 4B Woven with new Home Position of B–A

To achieve this Home Position, turn the cards one turn *Backward* from the normal Home Position of A–D, without filling, and start weaving from there. Notice that this design has reverse coloration from Figure 6-9a.

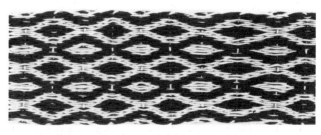

6-11a, b. Front and back of band, Pattern 40F.

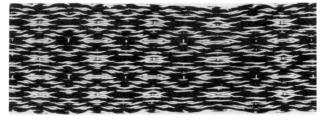

FANCY TURNING
Pattern 40G

Start in the normal Home Position, weave four turns Forward. Then, push Card 30 forward along the warp, ahead of the others. This should signal to you the onset of weaving with packets. Pass the filling through the shed as usual, turn Card 30 1F and Cards 1–29 1B. Clear the shed and pass the filling through. Push Card 29 forward, next to Card 30, and turn those two cards 1F and the rest of the cards (1–28) 1B. Clear the shed and continue weaving normally, but with each turn of the cards, take another card from the left and push it forward. Proceed until all the cards (including Card 1) have been advanced forward on the warp and turned Forward once.

While weaving, pay close attention to which card is the next to be moved forward. It is here that many mistakes occur. It is very easy to forget whether a turn has been completed—and it is even easier to make the same turn twice. Unlike normal 4F / 4B weaving, mistakes are very difficult to correct; usually trying to correct an error leads only to further complications.

The following detailed explanation of positioning is offered to help facilitate this procedure:

When Card 30 is turned Forward, it results in D–C being in the normally regarded Home Position. The rest of the cards 1–29, when turned Backward, result in B–A being in the position normally considered as Home. That is not to say that the Home Position is changed; it has not been altered. It means

6-12a, b. Front and back of band, Pattern 40G.

that the letter listed first is in the position that is normally occupied by A in the Home Position, and the letter listed second is in the relative position which is normally occupied by D when the cards are in the Home Position. This will be clearer in the explanation below:

1. Card 29 joins 30 and the result is:
30	D–C
29 et al	B–A

2. Cards 30 and 29 are turned 1F; Cards 1–28 are turned 1B. The result is:
30	C–B
29	A–D
28 et al	C–B

3. Cards 30, 29, and 28 are turned 1F; Cards 1–27 are turned 1B. The result is:
30	B–A
29	D–C
28	B–A
27 et al	D–C

4. Cards 30–27 are turned 1F; Cards 1–26 are turned 1B. The result is:
30	A–D
29	C–B
28	A–D
27	C–B
26 et al	A–D

As you can see, the cards will start to create an alternating symmetrical pattern. This will be one of the few guidelines available for the weaver to check if any one card is out of line with the others. All odd-numbered cards should be in the same relative position as should all even-numbered cards.

When all thirty cards have been turned Forward, the process repeats itself—only in reverse, starting with Card 1. Push the card forward this time ahead of the rest of the cards and pull the rest of the cards (2–30) back toward your body. Now, turn Card 1 1F and the large packet of cards 1B. Then, put Card 2 ahead with Card 1 and turn them 1F. The rest of the cards get turned 1B. The next card (3) joins 1 and 2, and in this way continue to Card 30. Weave all 30 cards 1F to complete the cycle and then, weave four turns (one full cycle) F to balance the design—this corresponds to the full cycle which was woven F in the beginning.

By now it is probably clear that as each card joins the forward packet it is in the same position (letterwise) as all the cards in that packet; the alternating regularity of the cards' positions has given way to consistent matching, so that all the cards end up in the same relative position.

Pattern 41 A–D
Warp Ends: 208
Warp Breakdown: 104 dark color
104 light color

This draft, unlike Figure 6-5, does not have a central core from which a symmetrical pattern radiates. Bearing this in mind, then, it should not be a surprise that the threading is all B-to-F. The diamonds, diagonals, and chevrons achieved from Pattern Draft 41 are all associated with Egyptian motifs (see Figure 6-23), and all have striking symmetry in common.

Remember, when weaving any intricate pattern, the design depends on the order of turning the cards. The weaver cannot, therefore, daydream.

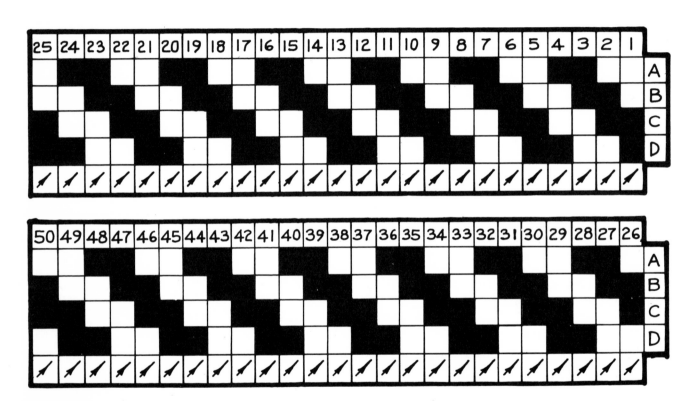

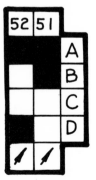

6-13. Draft for Patterns 41A-D.

It is wise to use a checklist of pattern steps or turning sequences against which to compare the woven segment. Although it is time-consuming, it is worth the effort to mark off from the list each segment as it is completed. When weaving any cycle as these, never, never stop in the middle.

Compare these diagonals with those achieved in Figure 5-37. The major difference is that in this case the "even" side remains on top—because the cards were turned in the prescribed direction to keep the even design on top.

Weave 4F / 4B until regular diagonal lines are showing on the band. After a neat, rhythmic pattern has developed, stop at Home Position and follow the directions for examples A through D.

Pattern 41A

1. Put filling through shed.
2. Push all the cards forward along the warp, *except* the last two, (51 and 52).
3. Turn Cards 51–52 1B.
4. Turn Cards 1–50 1F.
5. Clean the shed with a beater, but *do not pass the filling through the shed.*
6. Turn Cards 51–52 1B again.
7. Turn cards 1–50 1F again.
8. Clean the shed well and pass the filling through.
9. Take the next two cards, 49 and 50, from the packet on the right and slide them back down the warp to join 51 and 52.
10. Turn Cards 49–52 1B.
11. Turn Cards 1–48 1F.
12. Clean the shed well, but *do not pass the filling through the shed.*
13. Turn Cards 49–52 1B again.
14. Turn cards 1–48 1F again.
15. Clean the shed. Pass the filling through.
16. Continue this process until all the cards from the right-hand packet are in the left-hand packet; that is, until all the forward cards have been brought to the packet closer to your body. When Cards 1 and 2 join the rest, turn the entire packet 1B. Clean the shed, and turn *all* the cards 1B again. Pass the filling through the shed.

Remember, the filling does not pass through the shed at every turn of the cards, but rather after every two turns. It is imperative, however, that the shed be cleaned at each turn so that the pattern shows clearly. It is for this reason that the use of a beater is suggested.

This method of turning repeated many times produces the pattern shown in Figure 6-14b.

Repeat of Cycle A

Cycle A

6-14a, b. Pattern 41A, Cycle A, and repeats of Cycle A.

Pattern 41B

This pattern is the "flip" of Pattern 41A and is achieved by the reverse process: (See Figure 6-15a, b.)

1. Pass the filling through the shed.
2. Starting at the right, push the first two cards, 1 and 2, forward along the warp. Turn them 1F.
3. Turn the rest of the cards, Cards 3–52, 1B.
4. Clean the shed.
5. Turn Cards 1 and 2 1F again.
6. Turn cards 3–52 1B again.
7. Clean the shed and pass the filling through.
8. Push 3 and 4 forward and turn Cards 1–4 1F.
9. Turn Cards 5–52 1B.
10. Clean the shed.
11. Turn Cards 1–4 1F again.
12. Turn Cards 5–52 1B again.
13. Clean the shed.
14. Pass the filling through the shed.
15. Continue this process until all the cards have joined the forward packet and are turned 1F.
16. Clean the shed.
17. Turn all the cards 1F again.
18. Pass the filling through the open shed.

Repeat of Cycle B

Cycle B

6-15a, b. Pattern 41B, Cycle B, and repeats of Cycle B.

Pattern 41C

1. Pass the filling through the shed.

2. Push the last two cards on the right, 1 and 2, back down the warp, near the completed weaving. Keep Cards 3–52 forward along the warp, as they will form the packet turning Forward.

3. Turn Cards 1–2 1B.

4. Turn Cards 3–52 1F.

5. Beat the new shed.

6. Turn Cards 1 and 2 1B again.

7. Turn cards 3–52 1F again.

8. Beat the new shed.

9. Pass the filling through the new shed.

10. Slide cards 3 and 4 back down along the warp to join Cards 1 and 2. Turn this packet 1B.

11. Turn Cards 5–52 1F.

12. Beat the new shed.

13. Turn Cards 1–4 1B again.

14. Turn Cards 5–52 1F again.

15. Beat the new shed.

16. Pass the filling through the new shed.

17. Continue taking two cards at a time from the left-hand packet, sliding them down the warp to join the right-hand packet, until the last two cards, 51 and 52, are with the rest. Then turn the entire packet of Cards, 1–52, 1B. Beat the new shed and then turn the cards 1B again. Beat the shed again and then pass the filling through it.

Pattern 41D

1. Pass the filling through the shed.

2. Push Cards 51 and 52 forward along the warp.

3. Turn Cards 51 and 52 1F.

4. Turn the rest of the Cards, 1–50, 1B.

5. Beat the shed.

6. Turn Cards 51 and 52 1F again.

7. Turn Cards 1–50 1B again.

8. Beat the new shed.

9. Pass the filling through the shed.

10. Add Cards 49 and 50 to Cards 51 and 52 in the forward packet and turn them all 1F.

11. Turn Cards 1–48 1B.

12. Beat the new shed.

13. Turn Cards 49–52 1F again.

14. Turn Cards 1–48 1B again.

15. Beat the new shed.

16. Pass the filling through the shed.

17. Again, as with the previous three cycles, continue until all the cards have joined the forward packet and have been turned 2 Forward turns. Beat the new shed and pass the filling through it.

6-17. Pattern 41D, Cycle D.

6-16. Pattern 41C, Cycle C.

All four cycles and their opening steps are given in Figure 6-18 for easy reference.

Very interesting and different effects are achieved merely by alternating various combinations of these cycles. (See Figures 6-19a through g)

A good way to experiment with the limitless possibilities of these cycles is to make small building blocks of each cycle on pieces of paper about 2 inches square. Use a light-colored paper and mark the diagonal lines with a dark, wide magic marker. Be certain to indicate the top of each piece as well as the cycle letter. (You will soon discover that each piece is really the same pattern, turned forty-five degrees and this can be quite confusing.)

The two patterns shown in Figures 6-19d and e can be woven together to make one large diamond shape in the middle of the band. To weave these two patterns as one band, follow the step-by-step directions presented below. They are, of course, based on Pattern 41, but are given here for only twenty cards. (See Figure 6-20)

6-18. Cycles A through D of Pattern 41.

Cycle A
Left Packet	Right Packet
Cards 52-51 2B	Cards 1-50 2F
Cards 52-49 2B	Cards 1-48 2F
Cards 52-47 2B	Cards 1-48 2F
etc.	etc.

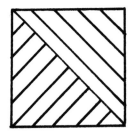

Cycle B
Left Packet	Right Packet
Cards 52-53 2B	Cards 1-2 2F
Cards 52-5 2B	Cards 1-4 2F
Cards 52-7 2B	Cards 1-6 2F
etc.	etc.

Cycle C
Left Packet	Right Packet
Cards 52-3 2F	Cards 1-2 2B
Cards 52-5 2F	Cards 1-4 2B
Cards 52-7 2F	Cards 1-6 2B
etc.	etc.

Cycle D
Left Packet	Right Packet
Cards 52-51 2F	Cards 1-50 2B
Cards 52-49 2F	Cards 1-48 2B
Cards 52-47 2F	Cards 1-46 2B
etc.	etc.

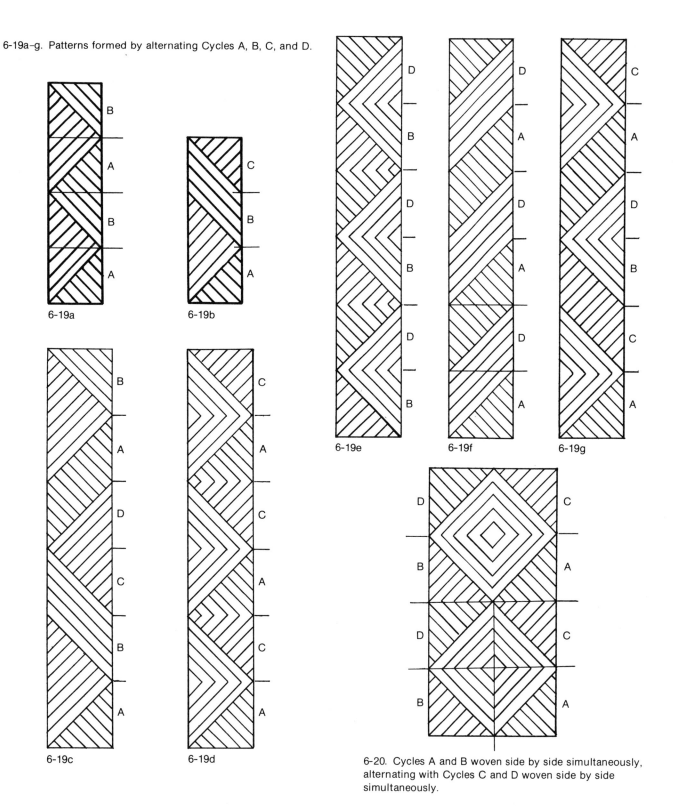

6-19a–g. Patterns formed by alternating Cycles A, B, C, and D.

6-19a

6-19b

6-19c

6-19d

6-19e

6-19f

6-19g

6-20. Cycles A and B woven side by side simultaneously, alternating with Cycles C and D woven side by side simultaneously.

There are several minor changes in the starting directions for this design, one of which is the use of filling with *every* turn of the cards. This is done because there are several packets turning in different directions at the same time and using a filling with each turn of the cards helps keep the pattern tightly packed. It elongates the diamond shape slightly, but does not distort it.

Remember, each half of the band is comprised of two different cycles—a total of four different cycles: Cards 1–10 represent alternating cycles of A and C. Cards 11–20 represent alternating cycles of B and D. Since each cycle divides the cards into two packs, there will now be a total of four packets along the warp, turning in alternate directions.

First, Cycles A and B are woven. When they are complete, Cycles C and D are woven. Proceed *very carefully* with the following directions:

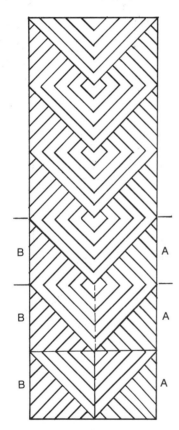

6-21. Repeats of Cycle A together with repeats of Cycle B, side by side.

1. Weave Forward until diagonal lines appear. Keep a record of the number of turns you do here, (a multiple of four is preferable and as few as four or eight are sufficient) so that at the completion of the diagonal, you can weave the same number of turns in reverse order to remove the tangles at the far end of the loom.

2. When the cards have returned to the Home Position, divide them into two packets—Cards 1–10 as one packet and Cards 11–20 as the other.

3. Turn Cards 1–10 1F. *This gets them in position to start the diamond.*

4. Feed the filling through the open shed.

5. Turn the cards as follows:

Cards 1–10	1F
Cards 11–20	1B

6. Feed the filling through the shed.

7. Repeat Step 5.

8. Feed the filling through the shed.

9. Next turn the cards as follows:

1–8	1F
9–10	1B
11–12	1F
13–20	1B

As you do this, position the cards along the warp in four packets, to facilitate turning them and to help you remember which packets are turning in which directions.

10. Feed the filling through the shed.

11. Repeat Step 9.

12. Feed the filling through the new shed.

13. Add two more cards to each of the smaller, middle packets from the larger, end packets and turn the cards thusly:

1–6	1F
7–10	1B
11–14	1F
15–20	1B

14. Feed the filling through the new shed.

15. Repeat Step 13.

16. Feed the filling through the shed.

17. Add two more cards to the two middle packets from the two end packets and turn the cards thusly:

1–4	1F
5–10	1B
11–16	1F
17–20	1B

18. Feed the filling through the new shed.

19. Repeat Step 17.

20. Feed the filling through the shed.

21. Add two more cards to the two middle packets from the two end packets and turn the cards thusly:

    1–2   1F
    3–10   1B
    11–18   1F
    19–20   1B

22. Feed the filling through the new shed.

23. Repeat Step 21.

24. Feed the filling through the shed.

25. Add the last two cards from each end packet to each middle packet. Turn the cards thusly:

    1–10   1B
    11–20   1F

26. Feed the filling through the new shed.

27. Repeat Step 25.

28. Feed the filling through the shed.

The bottom half of the diamond shape is now completed. (See Figure 6-20) To weave the top half, the directions must be reversed. These directions are listed very simply below. *Do not forget to pass the filling through the shed before each turn of the cards.*

1. 1–10   1F
   11–20 1B
2. Repeat Step 1.
3. 1–2   1B
   3–10   1F
   11–18 1B
   19–20 1F
4. Repeat Step 3.
5. 1–4   1B
   5–10   1F
   11–16 1B
   17–20 1F
6. Repeat Step 5.
7. 1–6   1B
   7–10   1F
   11–14 1B
   15–20 1F
8. Repeat Step 7.
9. 1–8   1B
   9–10   1F
   11–12 1B
   13–20 1F
10. Repeat Step 9.
11. 1–10   1B
   11–20 1F
12. Repeat Step 11.

Do not forget to remove the tangles which were created at the outset of this pattern series, in Step 1, prior to weaving Cycles A and B. If you made note of the number of turns that you wove forward, now weave the same number backward. That gives the diamond shape rather an attractive border as well. Patterns 65 through 75 are also reminiscent of Egyptian designs and are all ideal for experimentation with new turning sequences.

6-22. The patterns of these two bands were achieved with different combinations of the Cycles in Figure 6-18. Can you identify the various cycles?

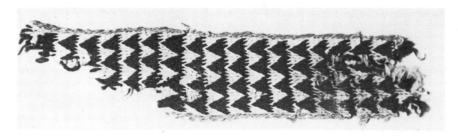

6-23. A fragment of an Egyptian card-woven band with horizontal rows of arrowheads—blue on a white ground with a red border. (Museum für Völkerkunde und Schweizerisches Museum für Volkskunde, Basel, Switzerland)

7. Fancy Weaves and Advanced Techniques

The draft in Figure 7-1 is used basically for two involved turning patterns, namely the Icelandic double weave and the Arabian double-faced weave. The pattern is simple and, if woven traditionally 4F / 4B would result in vertical stripes. (See Pattern 13.) Any number of cards could be used, and they can be threaded in one direction, in symmetric pairs, or in overall symmetry.

ARABIAN WEAVE
Pattern 42

With the cards in their normal Home Position, weave 2F / 2B, repeat. In this fashion the dark color will be on the top of the band. This turning method is what makes the fabric double-faced. By turning 4F / 4B, the light color is brought up to the top of the band, while the dark color goes to

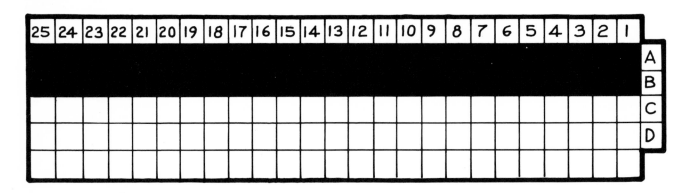

25	24	23	22	21	20	19	18	17	16	15	14	13	12	11	10	9	8	7	6	5	4	3	2	1	
																									A
																									B
																									C
																									D

7-1. Model two-color draft for the Icelandic and Arabian weaves, Pattern 42, which enables weaver to produce interesting designs, inscriptions, etc., in reverse coloration on each side—or simply a band with a different solid color on each side.

the underside. Many checkerboard effects can be achieved by dividing the cards into numerous packets and giving each a different turning sequence.

The bands in Figures 7-2 through 7-6 are all woven from this draft. Complicated inscriptions can be achieved from this threading pattern. To weave lettering, however, both extreme patience and expertise are required. With this in mind, consider some of the intricate bands reproduced in Chapter 1 as well as those which serve as chapter markers.

7-2. A typical example of the most common types of design achieved with the two-color draft for the double-faced weave. This specimen is from the Caucasus. Part of the band shows the underside with the dark pattern on the light ground. (Museum für Völkerkunde und Schweizerisches Museum für Volkskunde, Basel, Switzerland)

7-3. A spectacular religious book tie in the double-faced technique. The Sanskrit inscription consists of sacred texts, invocations to the gods, etc. The piece, dating from early 19th century India, is magenta and white silk, with gold threads marking the divisions in the text. (Victoria and Albert Museum, London, England, Crown Copyright)

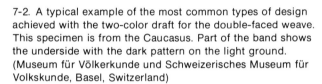

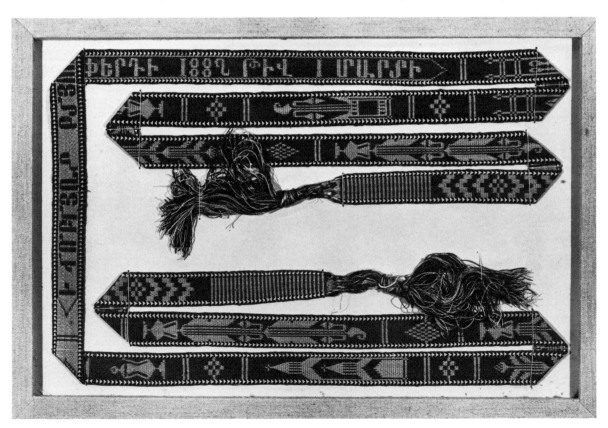

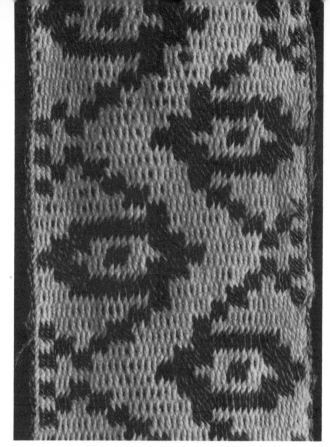

7-4. A Bulgarian sash in the double-faced technique. (Collection Hamburgisches Museum für Völkerkunde, Hamburg, Germany)

7-6. A most extraordinary piece in double-faced weave from Denmark, woven in the 1930s. This fabric was used as an altar decoration for a church. (Danish Museum of Decorative Art, Copenhagen)

7-5. A detailed close up of the other side of the band shown in Figure 7-4. The stitches twist when more than two turns are made in either direction with any card. When the 2F / 2B turning is maintained, the stitches are "straight" (i.e., do not slant to either direction) and the same color remains on the surface. (Collection Hamburgisches Museum für Völkerkunde, Hamburg, Germany)

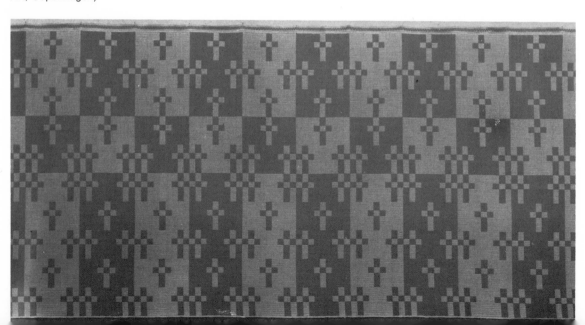

ICELANDIC DOUBLE WEAVE

The Icelandic style of weaving this draft also produces many patterns. This method, however, produces a true double weave, because with each turn of the cards, the filling is passed through the warp twice. This is not so impossible as it sounds, for the cards are woven unconventionally, on an angle, as in Figure 7-7. The filling passes from right to left through the top shed and then back again from left to right through the bottom shed.

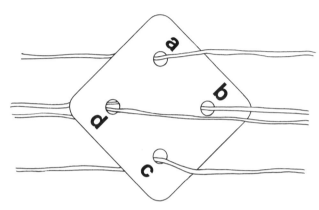

7-7. A card on an angle in order to weave in the Icelandic double-weave style.

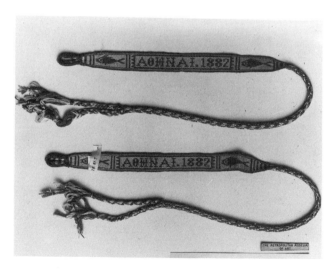

7-8. A Greek garter or brace, woven from a two-color draft for double weave, one end of which is a tubular weave. The band is blue and white silk with the inscription "At Athens—1882." (The Metropolitan Museum of Art, Gift of Mrs. Edward Robinson, 1920)

TUBULAR WEAVE

To weave a tubular band, as in Figures 7-8 through 7-10, begin with the cards in the regular weaving position, not on an angle as in the Icelandic Double Weave. Put the filling through from right to left where you wish the tubular weave to begin. Turn the cards and put the filling through the shed from *right to left* again by passing it over the top of the band. Turn the cards as usual and then pull the filling firmly. This will start to bring the two side edges of the band together to form a hollow tube. Again the filling is on the left, brought over the top of the band to the right, and inserted through the shed from right to left. Turn the cards and pull the filling securely. After two or three shots, the flat ends of the band are fastened together and the beginning of the tube is visible.

7-9. An example of tubular weave.

Consider making several tubular shapes on a single band of several inches in width. They could be placed at various intervals along the band, or all could be woven at the same point on the band, by dividing the cards into groups. To weave several tubular shapes at the same time requires additional filling—one for each tubular section. They could be started consecutively, so that their curved ends form a diagonal design . . . and so on. The possibilities are limitless.

Tubular weaves are most successful when all the cards are threaded in the same direction and woven without turn reversals. When removed from the loom, they have a tendency to spiral. This tendency will be quite apparent if you weave the tube from a horizontal stripe pattern; the stripe(s) will spiral around the tube.

SWEDISH WEAVE

This technique unlike the previous ones, is relatively simple to weave, as there are no complicated turning procedures. What makes this weave special is that one or more holes is left unthreaded and it is for this reason that the resulting weave is most interesting. The woven band has the look that repoussé and chasing give to metal. This is an exceptional style for thick or coarse fibers. The textures produced become part of the pattern.

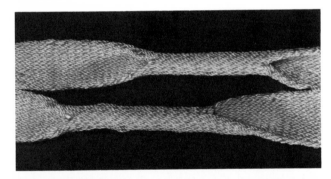

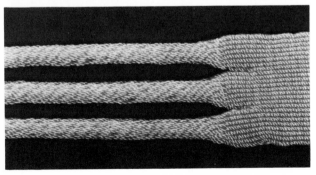

7-10a, b, c. Three very simple methods of using tubular weave in sections along a band.

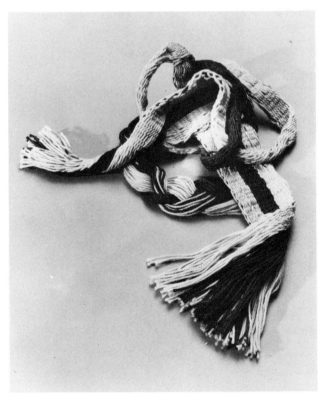

7-11. Tubular weave employed to make a little "sculpture." Can you identify the four different places tubular weave has been employed?

This is because those holes from which warp ends are omitted are an integral part of the design; they are not chosen at random.

The draft in Figure 7-12 (Pattern 43) is for just such a pattern. The boxes left blank in the pattern indicate those holes which are to be left *empty*. Most patterns that call for this type of threading do not utilize more than two or three colors in the pattern. This is done to keep the actual design simple, so that the texture, resultant from the thread-

Pattern 43

7-12. Draft for a Swedish weave, Pattern 43.

25	24	23	22	21	20	19	18	17	16	15	14	13	12	11	10	9	8	7	6	5	4	3	2	1	
R		B	B	B	B	B		R	R	R	B	B	B				B	B	B		R	R	R	R	A
R	B		B	B	B		B	R	R	R	B	B			B	B		B	B		R	R	R	R	B
R	B	B		B	B		B	B	R	R	R	R	B		B	B	B	B		B	R	R	R	R	C
R	B	B	B			B	B	B	R	R	R	R		B	B	B	B	B	B		R	R	R	R	D
↙	↙	↙	↙	↙	↘	↙	↘	↙	↘	↙	↘	↙	↘	↙	↘	↙	↘	↘	↙	↙	↙	↙	↙	↙	

50	49	48	47	46	45	44	43	42	41	40	39	38	37	36	35	34	33	32	31	30	29	28	27	26	
R	R	B	B			B	B	B	R	R	R		B	B	B	B	B				R	R	R	R	A
R	R	B	B		B	B		B	B	R	R	R	B		B	B	B	B		B	R	R	R	R	B
R	R	B		B	B	B	B		B	R	R	R	R	B	B		B	B		B	B	R	R	R	C
R	R		B	B	B	B	B	B		R	R	R	R	B	B	B			B	B	B	R	R	R	D
↘	↘	↘	↘	↘	↘	↙	↙	↙	↙	↙	↙	↙	↙	↙	↙	↙	↙	↙	↘	↘	↘	↘	↘	↘	

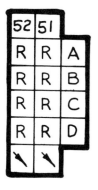

52	51	
R	R	A
R	R	B
R	R	C
R	R	D
↘	↘	

7-13. An example of Swedish weave, achieved with a simple diagonal pattern. The omission of warp ends in this solid-colored band creates the relief design, similar to an intaglio.

ing is rendered as the most interesting aspect of the band. Too complicated and colorful a design would detract from the Swedish weave. Leaving one hole empty in each card also means that there are one quarter fewer warp ends than usual and, therefore, less opportunity for a complicated multi-colored pattern.

Variety in Swedish weaves can be achieved also by using a filling which is heavier than the warp. This produces an outline of the filling on the surface of the band. This is also successful when only two holes in the card are filled. Threading only two holes in the card—that is, the *same* two holes in each card as A and D, for example—produces a plain, or tabby, weave and is particularly effective if all three elements (the filling and two sets of warp ends) are of different colors.

WEAVING WITHOUT FILLING

Another technique, which is not difficult at all, but which gives a very interesting effect involves omitting shots of filling. Turning the cards without the filling results in a loose, open weave; the warp ends twist over one another, but are never secured in place. Similarly, the warp ends from each card remain unconnected to the warp ends from each of the other cards.

Any pattern draft may be used to experiment with this technique, which can be worked at random or regular intervals. There are many, many ways to use this technique: for an inch or more, weave one half of the width of the band with filling and the other half without filling. Then switch, using filling on the half where you didn't use it before. This gives a checkerboard effect, with one side having a blurred, less delineated design, and the other having a regularly defined pattern. This effect is just as interesting with solid weaves as it is with patterned bands.

Color Plate C-12 shows two bands woven from Pattern 59. The band on the left shows how the pattern comes up when woven 8F / 8B. Notice the amazing difference between the two bands. While the pattern on the left is very definite and predictable, the pattern on the right is blurred. The band on the right is also wider because it does not have a filling thread to keep it fastened securely as a single unit.

To produce a band in this fashion, weave regularly, following the turning directions, to the point where you wish to drop off the filling. Turn the cards Forward or Backward the desired number of turns without the filling, beating every turn or two, to keep the rows of weaving fairly even. To reconnect the filling to the band, start from the point where the filling was left hanging and wrap it once or twice around the four warp ends of the last card on the left or right, depending which side the filling is on. It will not interfere with the pattern if the borders are solid and the filling is the same as the borders. Even if this is not the case, there will be no problem so long as the filling is one of the colors used in the border.

FRINGING THE SELVAGES

One form of fringing, which creates an interesting effect, is shown in Color Photo C-13, along the ends of the belts, but there are many ways to fringe the *selvages* of the bands as well.

Fringing along the selvage edge with loop fringing is shown in Figure 9-14b. To achieve this type of fringing, weave with either a pencil or dowel attached to one edge of the weaving to keep the fringe uniform. To do this, simply tape the object to be used to the hanger (or to the warp itself) and weave normally. When the filling is brought out at the side of the band, loop it around the dowel and bring it back through the shed, and out the other side. A dowel twelve inches long is adequate—as the weaving progresses the dowel can be moved up the side of the warp, leaving about five or six loops to hold it in place; it will then be in place for weaving the rest of the warp. Use one constant object to keep the size of the fringe consistent. Gauging by eye is inaccurate and sloppy.

If it is desired, the loops can be cut to form un-looped fringe; there is, however, always the danger of loosening the weave and even losing the filling. To prevent this, it is advisable to fasten the fringe at the selvage. To do this cut the filling into pieces as opposed to putting up many yards for filling on a shuttle. Each piece should be at least three times the width of the band, and longer, if long fringe is desired. Put a cut piece through the shed; turn the cards normally and bring it back to the side whence it originated. Tie the two ends together in a double knot and leave hanging. Continue weaving in this fashion until the desired length of fringing along the band is achieved, and cut the ends to a uniform length. If you fringe the entire length of the band this process is somewhat time-consuming, but the result is well worth the effort.

To fringe *both* selvages, the same process is used, but alternate the side from which the cut filling piece starts. Looping is not satisfactory because it is not tight enough and the warp ends would slide from side to side along the filling shots and ultimately result in a loose mélange of twisted warp ends.

This method allows for fringe at every other shot of filling, along either one or both selvages. If, however, a fuller look is desired, then another method is used for fringing. The filling which will be used to make the fringe must again be cut into pieces. Each length should be equal to slightly more than the width of the band plus twice the length of the fringe desired. For example, if two

inch fringe is desired for a band three inches wide, cut each piece about eight inches long. Pass one piece through the shed normally, distributing the excess five inches evenly at both edges, about two and one-half inches at each selvage. Turn the cards and beat the new shed. Take another eight-inch piece, pass it through the new shed, again turn the cards, and beat the new shed. Then, at each selvage, tie the two pieces together. If thicker fringe is desired, pass two filling pieces through each shed, thus doubling the amount of fringe, but also increasing the thickness of the band.

BEADING

Attaching beads to the edges of a band can also add a new dimension to the finished piece. This can be done in several fashions:

1. Sew them on after the piece is finished, using the filling fiber for "thread." That way it will match and not show along the selvage.

2. Weave them onto the band by using cut pieces for the filling (instead of a continuous one) knotting them as above.

3. Weave them to the band, by putting the filling through the hole in the bead with each shot. In this case, it is good to work with several shorter pieces for filling rather than one long one.

7-14. Two types of fringing are shown here, both executed with a filling much heavier than the warp. Because of this difference in the two fiber weights, no dowel was needed to make the naturally occurring "loops" of filling along the selvages; likewise, the long individual pieces of filling are held tightly in place by the thin warp cutting into the larger, more lush filling fiber.

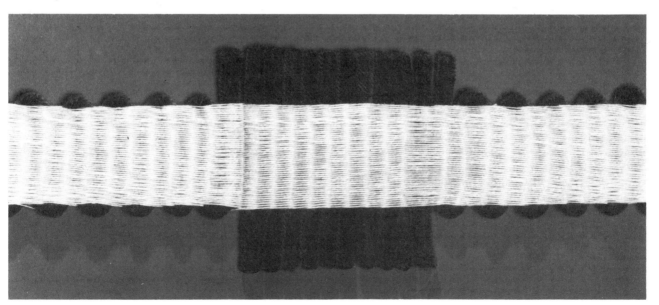

SLITS

This technique involves weaving one band with a "slit" in it every so often. The slits can be used as a means of heightening interest in a pattern or for more functional purposes—such as the button-holes on the band adorning the sweater in Color Plate C-19 or for the belt-buckle holes.

To weave one band as two (which is actually what is being done), insert a second filling before the point where the separation is desired. This second filling does not have to be nearly so long as the first, but certainly should be of the same color and fiber. Put it through the shed in the opposite direction from the original. Weave both fillings together through the new shed, even though they are going in opposite directions. This is done not only to secure the second filling in the band, but also to reinforce the band at a point where there will be greater than usual stress. It further prevents loosening, unravelling, or even breakage.

After weaving two shots with the two fillings, divide the packet of cards where you wish the division to be, and set the two packets slightly apart from each other along the warp. Put the filling on the right through the shed created by the cards on the right and bring it out to the top of the band after the last card in the packet. Do the same with the filling from the left-hand packet. Turn both packs of cards, to change the two sheds, and beat the two new sheds. Before putting either filling through the new sheds, loop one around the other, as in Figure 7-15. Then return each filling through the two new sheds; the filling that originated at the right will be back there, as will the left be back at the left side of the band. This looping acts as a final measure to keep this delicate point secure, and is particularly necessary if the slit is being made for buttonholes.

Now, weave the right-hand packet following your pattern and using only the filling on the right. To make it easier to weave, and to avoid catching warp ends from the left-hand packet, push the second packet up along the warp out of reach.

After completing the weaving with the right-hand pack, push it up out of the way and bring the left-hand packet toward you. Now pull on the filling in this pack to take the slack out of the loop created earlier. Continue weaving the left-hand pack a com-

mensurate number of turns as the right-hand pack. Weave with the same rhythm and tension. This is important so that both bands end at the same place along the warp; the amount of weaving should be even, so the two sides can be joined together again to form one band.

To rejoin the two bands into one, the same procedure is followed as was used before the slit. Be sure to include the overlapping of both fillings for two or three shots to strengthen the area. It is advisable to also loop the two fillings as directed before. After the piece has been successfully rejoined, continue weaving with the original filling.

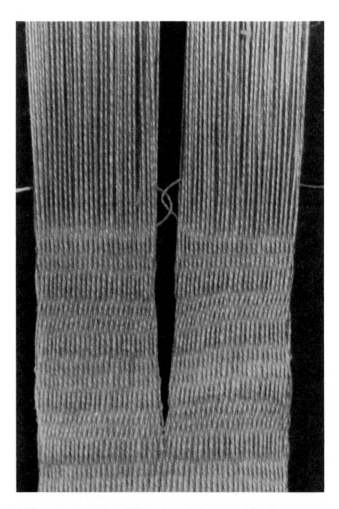

7-15. Interlocking two fillings for reinforcement for the buttonholing technique.

If the second filling has been worked through several sheds and has been looped as recommended, there is no fear of unravelling, and the extra filling may simply be cut off at the point where it is dangling from the selvage.

This technique can be used to form many bands from one band and is not necessarily confined to buttonholing, as illustrated with the two bands in Color Plate C-21. As mentioned, this technique is based on the process used to obtain buttonholes. With this in mind, consider the illustration. At first glance, these bands appear to be sophisticated pieces of card weaving; considering however the principle on which they are based, they are really nothing more than segments of one band intermittently braided together.

To break one large band up into segments for braiding, follow the directions used for buttonholing. If, however, one band is going to be separated into more than three or four bands for braiding, do not bother with the looping and reinforcing. Simply insert a new filling for each band segment and leave an end long enough to rework back into the weaving. Methods for finishing loose ends are discussed in Chapter 8.

Weave each individual band-section the necessary length. Only then, is it advisable to braid the bands. Gently place each packet in its new position and continue weaving. This technique works especially well with borders (as shown in Color Plate C-21), or small motifs crisscrossed over a band.

FLOATING

"Floating" the filling over several warp ends on the surface of the band gives another interesting effect similar to brocading. This is very simple to do and any arrangement works well; it looks infinitely more intricate to the eye than it is for the hand. (See Figures 7-16 and 7-17.) Similarly, warp ends can be floated over the filling by not turning all the cards at one time. The cards which hold the warp ends you desire to float, should remain in position while the others are turned; they can be floated for as many turns as desired.

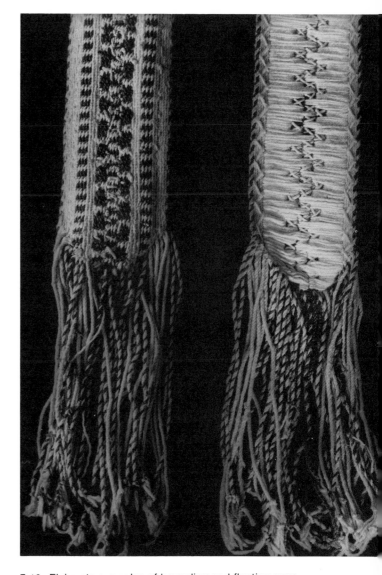

7-16. Elaborate examples of brocading and floating were incorporated into this Bulgarian belt (front and back shown here). The warp ends are twisted together in clusters and knotted at the ends. (Collection Hamburgisches Museum für Völkerkunde, Hamburg, Germany)

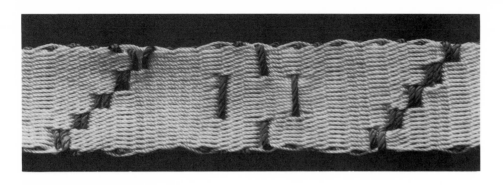

7-17. Three very simple examples of floating filling over the
warp. This technique looks particularly interesting with a filling
of a different color and texture from the warp.

8. Finishing Touches/ Pieces to Make

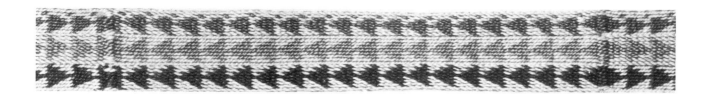

SECURING THE FILLING

With both loose ends of filling secured to the top of the band (as discussed in Chapter 4) disengage both ends of the loom from the stationary objects and remove the elastic band near the cards. Gently untangle any twists that are in the warp ends and slide the cards off the remaining length of unwoven warp. Untape the loose filling at this end of the band so that you can secure it by "reweaving" with a large tapestry needle. Once this end is rewoven then, and only then, should you untie the fastening and remove the filling taped to the band at the other end of the loom. Remember, these are security measures, to prevent the ends from unravelling and the width of the band from splaying out.

8-1. Filling being reworked in center of the band.

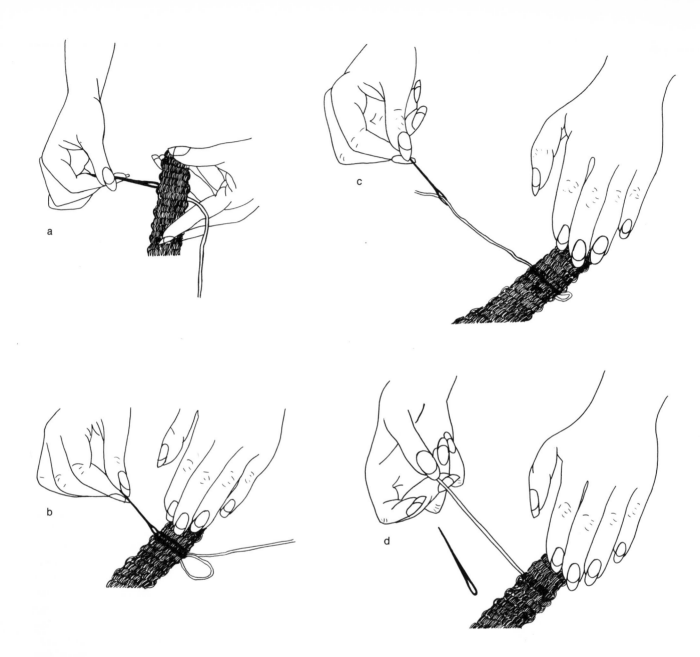

8-2. To secure an unbound end of the filling (a) insert a tapestry needle, eye first, into a row of weaving adjacent to the loose end. Push the needle through to the other side of the band, thread the loose filling in the eye of the needle (see Fig. 8-1), and then bring the needle back to the side from which it originated (b) taking the loose filling with it. Continue to pull the loose filling, bringing it all the way to the other side (c). You can remove the needle and pull the filling itself. Take up the excess, so that a loop is created. The loop will ultimately appear as another filling stitch along the selvage and will hardly be notice-able (d). To be certain that the filling will not unravel, insert the needle through the next row of weaving and repeat this procedure. Note: at the beginning and end of the band, there is only one possible row through which the needle can go; at points along the middle of the band, there can be two rows. Generally, however, because there are usually two loose ends that need to be rewoven into the band (see Fig. 8-1), it is best to reweave them in opposite directions, away from each other. For purposes of clarity, only one loose end of filling along the middle of the band is illustrated here.

For reweaving the filling, choose a needle that is longer than the width of the band whenever possible. Generally, a three-inch needle is adequate, with both the eye and the point ends rounded and dull. With a gentle, turning motion, put the *eye* end of the needle through the next to the last *closed* shed of the weaving so that the eye comes out at the selvage where the loose filling is. If the loose filling end has been brought through the last (open) shed of the band from left to right, then the *eye* of the needle must also end up on the right. Leave the needle in the weaving so that both its ends (the eye and the point) are exposed at the selvages of the band. Thread the filling through the eye, and then pull the needle back to its original position on the left side of the band.

Repeat this procedure, this time putting the needle through (eye first) from the right to the left, as the loose end is now on the left. The needle should be put through the row of weaving adjacent to the loose filling. This row of weaving is the next to the last row of completed weaving. After two or three times the filling should be secure, and the excess cut off close to the selvage of the band. (If the band is fringed, then it can be left as part of the fringe.) If you want to ensure that the cut end remains in place, put a dab of clear-drying glue at the selvage.

Repeat this same process to secure the filling at the other end of the band. This procedure results in double shots of filling through the first and last few sheds on the band and will make the band slightly thicker, but otherwise, will not affect the weaving.

If there are loose ends of filling along the length of the band (because several short filling pieces were used), then, they, too, can be reworked back through the weaving in this fashion. Remember that along the woven band, any place a new filling was started there will be two loose ends—the end of one filling and the beginning of another—and both must be reworked back into the band with a tapestry needle, working in opposite directions to avoid a bulky lump on the surface. If, however, each new filling was added in the overlapping manner described earlier, then the loose ends have already been secured and can simply be cut off at the selvage. Again, for extra protection against unravel-

ling, these cut ends can be held in place with a drop of glue.

Once the loose filling ends are secured, the band is ready to become something! There are many ways to finish the ends, depending on the purpose for which the band was made. The simplest, of course, is to make a fringed belt.

FINISHING THE WARP ENDS

There is an endless variety of ways to finish off the loose warp ends of card weavings to give them a neat and professional look. Many are illustrated in photographs throughout this book.

Fringing the warp ends is a simple process, since the fringe is already a built-in feature of the band (i.e., the unwoven warp at both ends). Secure the filling at the far end of the belt as described above. Before securing the filling at the beginning, inspect the first few rows of weaving. Chances are the cards probably did not produce a very even weave until a good turning rhythm was established when the weave developed even selvages and regular "stitches."

If this end looks uneven and messy, it is wise to "unweave" the imperfect segment. If a heading was used for just this purpose, now is the time to take it out. Both the normal filling and/or a heading are removed in the same fashion, with the aid of a tapestry needle. The loose end of the filling on the right, is free to go through the warp ends and then dangle on the left. Leaving it on the left, look along the right-hand selvage for the point where the filling shows. Using the eye of the needle, gingerly tug the looped filling so it comes through the warp out to the right side. Again, insert the needle through the next loop of filling which will be showing at the left-hand side of the band and pull to get the end through. Continue this process of releasing the filling from alternating sides of the band until all the uneven weaving, or the entire heading, has been removed. If the weaving has formed "ribs" in the warp, it may be necessary to steam the fringe. Then, "reweave" the loose filling end through the woven band as described above.

Fringe looks best if all the fibers are of approximately the same length. It tends to look sloppy if left too ragged. Cut the ends to the desired length and voilà! A finished sash.

A band woven to a point, highlighted by fringe around it, is a simple technique to achieve. When the desired length of band has been woven, omit the outermost cards on each selvage on the next turn of the cards. With each successive turn, omit another card from each edge so that those warp ends are neither turned nor woven.

Knotting each warp end gives a professional look to the fringe, particularly with thick fibers. (See the middle belt in Color Plate C-13). This is particularly true with multi-ply fibers, because below the knot the fiber can frizz up and add a new dimension to the band. Knotting is not, however, a good idea with thin fibers—unless several warp ends are knotted together either at their ends or an inch or so from them.

Beads can effectively be added to fringe to greatly enhance a belt. Put the beads either at the end of the warps or an inch or so from the ends. (See Color Plate C-13 where the plies of the warp

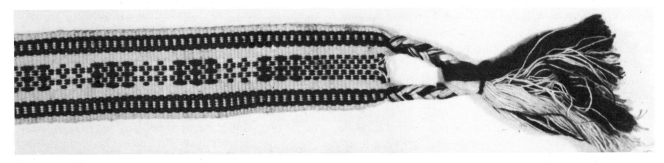

8-3. Braiding warp ends can add a new dimension to the woven band. The Swedish ribbon here is an apron tie. (Collection Hamburgisches Museum für Völkerkunde, Hamburg, Germany)

8-4. One end of this Persian silk is braided; the other has a tubular weave (at the rolled-up end) which enables a self-closure. (The Museum of History, Berne, Ethnographical Department)

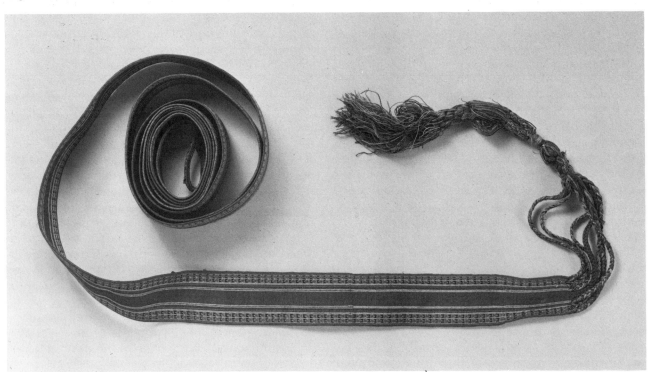

have unravelled below the beads.) In some cases, two warp ends per bead may be necessary.

Braiding the fringe (as in Figures 8-3 and 8-4) creates a beautiful colorful look and is simple to do. Any number of warp ends can be braided in any combination.

Banding is a process used professionally to unite "clumps" of fringe ends into one tassle. One or several bands can be made from the warp ends. (See Figures 8-5 and 8-6.) To achieve this wrapped look use the longest warp end from the fringe. If the decision to band the fringe has been made at the time of warping, then one warp end can be cut extra long for this purpose. The filling can also be used for banding after it has been worked back into the weaving, if it is long enough.

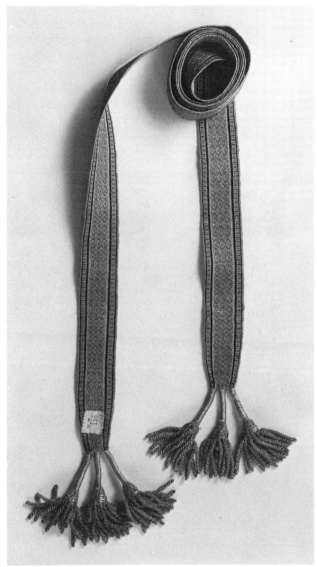

8-5 and 8-6. These banding techniques give a slightly different look. The warp ends of the Bulgarian tie in Figure 8-5 are wrapped quite colorfully. (Photo collection of the Hamburgisches Museum für Völkerkunde, Hamburg, Germany) The Persian band in Figure 8-6 has warp ends wrapped in gold filaments with elaborate tassels on the ends. (Museum of History, Berne, Ethnographical Department)

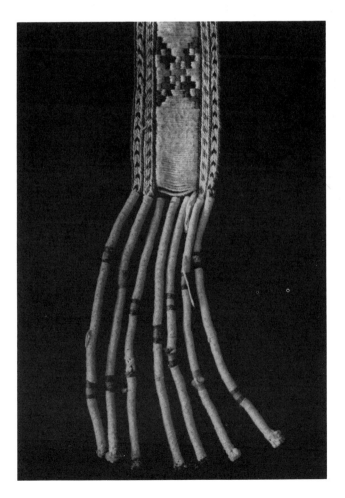

Figures 8-7a through j illustrate how to band the warp. Grasp the fringe bundle with index finger and thumb of the right hand at the point where the banding is to start. Take the longest end of warp or filling and hold it in your left hand. Bring it up around the index finger, making a loop. Remove your index finger from the loop. Holding the loop secure, start to wrap the banding fiber around the fringe packet so that it starts to cover the loop. Adjust the fingers of the right hand to hold the beginning of banding to keep it secure. Continue to wrap until the loop is almost covered. At that point, put the end of the banding piece *through* the exposed end of the loop. Holding the band with the right hand, grasp the rows of banding and give them a tug downward so that they cover the loop. In this way, the long end becomes a part of the fringe; its excess can be cut so that it is the same length as the fringe.

Macramé is another excellent technique to use

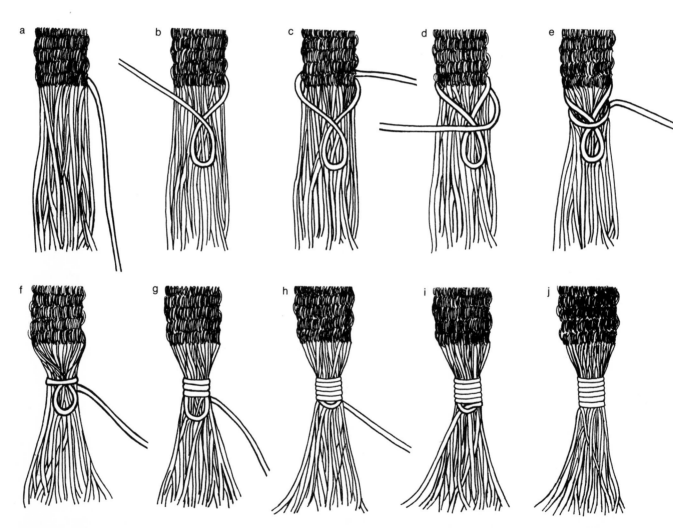

8-7a to j. To band the filling: A loop (b) is created with this end and brought around the back of the band (c) to its starting point. The filling is then brought around the band again (d) and tightened a little (e) to start to bring the warp end together into one firm bundle (f). Continue wrapping this end around the warp ends, almost covering the loop (f, g). When only a bit of the loop is left uncovered (h), insert the end through the loop (i) and then tug the series of bandings down over the loop to secure it (j). The end will disappear as it becomes a part of the cluster of banded fringes.

for finishing warp ends. If you are familiar with this art, you will want to plan a long warp especially for this purpose. (See Color Plate C-7.)

There are no rules for combining card weaving with *belt buckles*—imagination, again, is the only limit. Figure 8-8 and Color Plates C-5 and C-14 illustrate just how much a particular belt buckle can add to a belt.

First select the style of closure to suit the purpose and the wearer and then select the buckle to be used. Any buckle that does not allow for size adjustment, like several shown in Figure 8-8, creates problems. To adjust the size on these belts, then, either snaps or Velcro tabs were sewn on the inside of one end of the belt. The latter is the simpler means.

Two half rings is the simplest closure to use because it is self-adjustable, stays securely fastened, and is readily available at any five-and-ten-cent store. (See Figure 8-9.) To use this buckle, first

8-8. Many different types of buckles can be used to finish the ends of a woven belt.

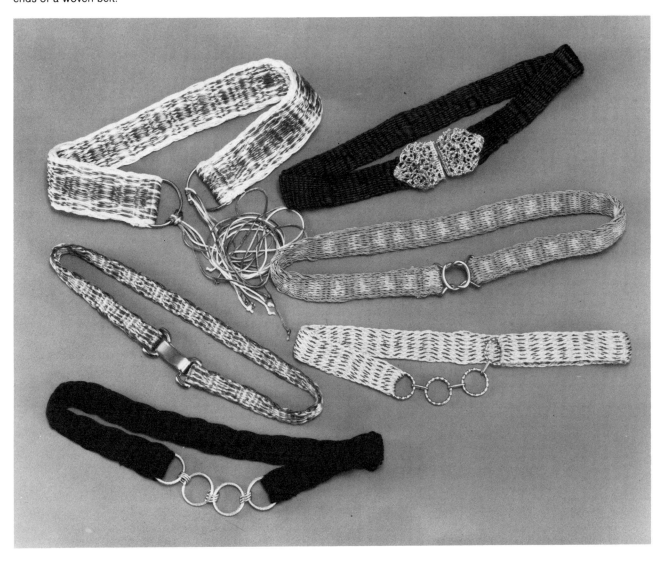

finish off ends of the band. Then determine how long the belt must be and whether any of the band need be cut off. Do *not* cut anything off, however, but simply mark the place where the band should be cut. Then, either by hand or machine, stitch across the width of the band—one-quarter to one-half inch away from the proposed cut. (Remember this stay stitching remains on the section of the band you are using, not on the discarded end.) The stitching helps keep the filling in place and prevents the end of the band, when cut, from widening. (A thin layer of glue can be put on the open warp, but this is not necessary.)

Next put the two half-rings in place and fold the band over to attach them. Be sure to fold it over in the proper direction so that the side you want showing *is outside*. Then, by hand, stitch this part of the band down in place. Because of the band's thickness, it is not necessary to sew all the way through to the front, and, therefore, the stitches will not be visible.

The other end of the belt can be finished in any way. The belt in Color Plate C-5 is stitched by machine across its face and then the ends cut and fringed. The black, gray, and white belt in Color Plate C-14 is finished as described above and covered on the end with a black ribbon to match the borders. The blue-and-yellow checked belt in Color Plate C-14 is thin enough to fold back on the inside and stitch in place.

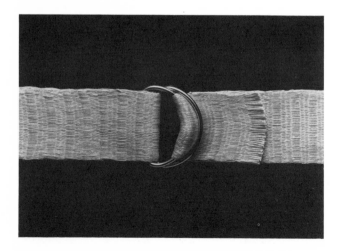

8-9. Two half, or "D," rings used for a simple belt buckle.

No matter what method is used to fasten a belt or finish the ends of a piece, think in terms of enriching the look of the band itself and adapting it for its function. For example, it would be senseless to make a place mat by joining several bands together with macramé. This would make a pretty wall hanging, but is impractical and flimsy for a place mat. That purpose can better be served by stitching together several bands.

PLACE MATS

A place mat (or set of place mats) can actually be woven so that there is little finishing work required once the warp comes "off the loom." Planning a set of four mats, each fourteen by twelve inches, involves a little arithmetic figuring, but is simple weaving. The theory behind it, naturally, is to join together panels of card weaving.

Decide first whether the place mats are to be of a solid color or design, whether more than one design or color scheme or several designs with several colors is desired, and whether each mat should be the same. Consider the necessary planning for these contingencies.

To make solid-colored place mats:
Size: twelve by fourteen inches with one inch-fringe along the two twelve-inch sides
Fiber: heavy linen
Width of band: 4 inches

Three woven strips (each four inches wide by fourteen inches long) will be needed to make each place mat. In addition, each piece will have to have fringe on both ends, which accounts for an extra six inches of warp. The length of the warp, then, must be at least forty-eight inches (three times fourteen plus six inches for fringe) for *one* place mat. Four place mats would require four times that, or one-hundred-ninety-two inches (five and one-third yards) plus about twelve inches for the unweavable ends, and at least another twelve inches for take up—a total of at least six yards for the put up. Six yards, or eighteen feet, is rather long for one band (do you have a room that long for weaving?), but it is easier to put up the warp and thread the cards only once. The warp can be combed and woven in segments, so it is not really so awesome as it looks and sounds.

After the entire length of warp has been woven, it must be cut up into lengths of sixteen inches (fourteen inches for the place mat and one inch each for the fringe on the two sides). Three sixteen inch bands are then stitched together to make the mat. The ends are then fringed. From the cutting they will have already started to unravel a bit—merely help them along with a tapestry needle by pulling the filling out to "unweave" the necessary one inch on each side. Remember to reweave the filling ends to secure them, if necessary.

For patterned place mats, many alternatives are open for the weaver. Pick a color scheme and work four different warps, each with a different design, each earmarked for one place mat. Or, with the same four patterns, make four place mats, each having one strip from each pattern. Another idea is to make the same pattern but in different colors for each mat. No matter what method is chosen, any set of hand-woven place mats brightens up a table and also creates an eye-catching conversation piece.

POT HOLDERS/HEADBANDS/BAG STRAPS/SHOELACES

Pot holders can be made in much the same way by stitching together two bands. They can even be made from one wide band—in a six- or eight-inch square. Machine stitching around the edges keeps the weaving secure. The ends can be fringed for a decorative finish.

The ends of a band to be used for a head band can be finished in much the same way the ends of a belt are finished. To make the headband adjustable, use snaps, Velcro tabs, or elastic. The latter is a good way to fashion a headband. Fold back the two ends of the band and stitch them in place. Then, put an elastic through the ends of the band and tie or stitch it down on one end, inside the band. A wide piece of elastic can be stitched to both ends of the band, without folding the ends of the band over.

Stitch the ends of bands to be used for pocketbook straps, also. The wide strap in Color Plate C-3 is not only used for the strap, but also for the sides of the pocketbook. Long, thin bands can be used for double straps, wrapped around a shoulder handbag on the front and rear panels.

CRAFT COMBINATIONS

Macramé can also be used to join panels of card weaving. The cords to be used for macramé can be anchored to the band at any point where the filling is exposed at the selvages. To do this, use a tapestry needle, threaded with the cord to be used for the macramé. Put the needle through the looped filling (showing along the selvage of the band). Naturally, this should be done after the card weaving is completed.

Crocheting and knitting are also other effective ways of binding pieces of card weaving together. Similarly, pieces can be joined by plaiting other fibers in a crisscross pattern between the two bands. The braiding can be anchored every inch or so with the aid of a tapestry needle—again through the exposed filling along the selvages.

Another finishing touch is combining gay embroidery—or even brocading—and card weaving. This particular practice was common in Church weavings—especially brocading with silver and/or gold threads—to adorn priests' maniples, as well as for embellishments for religious bookties.

Another technique is to combine card weaving with rug or fabric weaving (or almost any weaving on a "regular" loom). For example, card weaving can be combined with, and used as trim for a traditionally-woven shawl, by using the warp of the stole (which forms fringe) as the filling on the card weaving. Set up the card loom as usual, but instead of preparing filling for the warp, use the *fringed ends of the stole*. In this manner, the two *warps* are at right angles to each other. This creates a card-woven band directly *against* the woven edge of the shawl and complements the edge with a design.

A similar technique can be used to weave a band against the edges of a rug. In either case, be sure the warp ends of the loom-woven object are long enough to function as filling for the card weaving. Several warp ends can be woven together as a single filling for the band, and, likewise, can be left as fringe once they have been put through the band to secure the twisting action of the warp ends of the band.

9. Working on Your Own

Once you (1) are familiar with the three major stages of card weaving—setting up the loom, weaving the band, and finishing off the fabric—(2) can understand and weave drafts, and (3) are able to examine a draft and have some idea of how it will look when it is transferred from paper to fiber, then you are ready to proceed to the more elaborate patterns presented in this chapter and to begin to draft patterns of your own.

DRAFTING A DESIGN

Drafting is not nearly so complicated a procedure as you might expect. The first thing to do in planning any pattern is to make a grid on which to work. Number Card 1 on the right-hand side of the grid, since that is how the cards are set up on the loom. To draft the pattern itself, first use either letters or symbols in the blocks on the grid to represent the different yarns being used. After the draft is marked, fill in each block with the appropriate color which will later be threaded in the hole. This is done to give the weaver a rough idea of how the pattern will look when woven. Crayons, colored pencils, pentels, etc., are all good for this purpose. (Some weavers prefer to simply design the pattern from start with blocks of color and never use symbols or letters. Regardless of which method is chosen for drafting, however, it is al-

ways a good idea to check a draft for accuracy and design proportion by coloring in the blocks on the grid. What appears to be a perfect pattern in letters may be an unbalanced one in color.)

Next, enter the threading directions along the bottom of the draft. Finally, include a chart with each draft, showing the key to symbols, colors, etc.; and a breakdown of the warp ends, as those presented in this book, so that a pattern can be repeated without difficulty.

To see what the pattern will look like when the weaving is reversed (4F / 4B), place a mirror along the top edge of the draft, flush up against "row A." Eight rows of "stitches" materialize, complete with the turn reversal of the cards at the edge of the mirror.

UNDERSTANDING HOW DESIGNS DEVELOP

To understand how the mirror trick works, it is necessary to first fully comprehend the manner in which the cards function to give a design. Pattern 40 shows how the woven design can change form when the Home Position is changed. When weaving with the traditional Home Position at A–D, the A hole is on the upper edge (near the ceiling) in the far corner (away from the weaver). As the cards are turned Forward, the A hole goes down toward the floor. It is the warp end that is in that position (the upper-outer corner) which shows on the top of the band. This is true all the way along the band, from the first card to the last card—the color that is in the upper-outer corner is the color that will result in the next row of weaving. On the first turn of the cards, however, the A warp ends do not really result in a visibly woven row because there is no other warp end previously woven for the A warp end to twist around.

For the second turn of the cards, the D hole is in the upper-outer corner. When it is turned down toward the floor, the warp ends from the D holes can wrap around those from the A holes, resulting in a visible row of woven "stitches" across the width of the band.

The next hole in the key position is the C hole. When the cards are turned Forward, the warp ends from the C holes wrap around the previous D warp ends, and a row of stitches (representative of the warp ends in the C holes) appears across the width of the band.

After the C holes have been turned down, the B holes are in the key position and when they are turned down, they wrap around the warp ends from the C holes and also result in a row of stitching across the width of the band.

So far the cards have been turned four times and are now back in the Home Position. The resultant weaving from this full cycle is: One not-so-visible row of weaving (from the warp ends in the A holes of the cards); and, three perfect rows of woven "stitches" (from the warp ends in the D, C, and B holes, respectively).

Between the weaver and cards, the weaving appears thusly:
Unwoven warp ends
Cards
B row of weaving
C row of weaving
D row of weaving
(A) half-twists
Weaver

Now that the cards have returned to the Home Position, weave Forward again four turns. The A holes of the cards are in the key position, and this time, will result in a row of visible weaving. After this 1 turn Forward, the weaving will appear thusly:

Unwoven warp ends
Cards
A row of weaving
B row of weaving
C row of weaving
D row of weaving
(A) half-twists
Weaver

After *twelve* turns Forward (three full cycles of the cards), the band will appear:
Unwoven warp ends
Cards
B row of weaving
C row of weaving
D row of weaving
A row of weaving
B row of weaving
C row of weaving
D row of weaving
A row of weaving
B row of weaving
C row of weaving
D row of weaving
(A) half-twists
Weaver

That is how a pattern, woven with *all Forward turns* develops. This was explained briefly at the end of Chapter 5 under Diagonal Stripes. By placing an identical copy of a draft above its original you simulate the effect achieved by continuous Forward turns. If, however, the turning directions call for a turn reversal after four turns then the weaving develops along a different line.

First of all, the key position becomes the upper-inner corner (or the same relative position of the D hole when the cards are in Home Position). This is because the cards are now going to be turned Backward and it is that inner corner (nearer the weaver) which will be going down when the cards are turned.

Just as in the beginning, however, when the weaving was started in the Forward direction, and the first turn Forward did not really result in a distinct row of weaving, so, too, the first turn Backward does not really give a woven row of "stitches." This first turn Backward has nothing for the warp ends to cling to; without an anchor, these warp ends from the D holes cannot surface on the weaving as a row. These warp ends remain buried *inside* the band:

```
                Unwoven warp ends
                Cards
   1B      {(D) buried row of weaving
turn reversal - - - - - - - - - - - - - - - - - - - - - - - - - - - - - -
           ⎰B row of weaving
   4F      ⎱C row of weaving
            ⎰D row of weaving
            ⎱(A) half twists
                Weaver
```

Next, the A holes move into the key position in the upper-inner corner. The cards are turned Backward and all the warp ends in the A holes surface as the next row of weaving:

```
                Cards
   2B      ⎰A row of weaving
           ⎱(D) buried row of weaving
turn reversal - - - - - - - - - - - - - - - - - - - - - - - - - - - - - -
           ⎰B row of weaving
           ⎪C row of weaving
   4F      ⎪D row of weaving
           ⎱(A) half twists
                Weaver
```

The next set of holes in the key position is B. After the cards are turned, and the B holes go down, the warp ends in the B holes become a row of weaving on the band. Similarly, when the C holes assume the key position next, and are turned, they, too, become a row of weaving.

After two full cycles of turns (four turns Forward and four turns Backward) have been completed, the weaving will look like this:

```
                Cards
           ⎰C row of weaving
   4B      ⎪B row of weaving
           ⎪A row of weaving
           ⎱(D) buried row of weaving
turn reversal - - - - - - - - - - - - - - - - - - - - - - - - - - - - - -
           ⎰B row of weaving
   4F      ⎪C row of weaving
           ⎪D row of weaving
           ⎱(A) half twists
                Weaver
```

Notice that the "stitch" of the A row at the point of the turn reversal is slightly longer than all the rest. It is also "straighter" in that it doesn't slant to the right or to the left as do the other rows. This row is slightly longer because it actually stays on top of the band for two turns: (1) When the D holes are turned down and buried inside the weaving, and (2) when the A holes themselves are turned down from the key position. This A row of weaving is actually twice as long as the other rows because it *covers* the D row.

Now, the cards are back in the Home Position ready to start another Forward cycle. The A hole is once again in the key position (upper-outer corner, this time, for Forward turning). As these A warp ends get turned down, they cannot anchor onto the weaving because the direction of the turning is being changed. They are *buried* in the band and do not surface as a row of weaving. This is precisely what occurred to the D warp ends when they were turned down at the last turn reversal.

Next, the D holes in the key position get turned Forward and, as they go down, result in a row of weaving on the surface of the band. Just as the A holes resulted in a longer stitch during the last turn reversal, so do the warp ends in the D holes now result in a longer stitch.

Next, the C, and then the B holes come into the key position and as each gets turned down, results in a regular row of stitching on the band. The cards are then again back in Home Position, and the weaving on the band looks like:

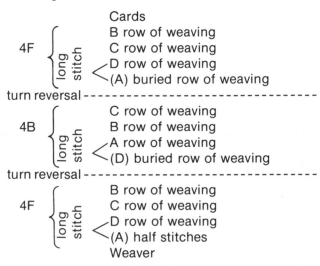

```
                Cards
           ⎰        B row of weaving
   4F      ⎪  long  C row of weaving
           ⎪ stitch <D row of weaving
           ⎱        <(A) buried row of weaving
turn reversal - - - - - - - - - - - - - - - - - - - - - - - - - - - - - -
           ⎰        C row of weaving
   4B      ⎪  long  B row of weaving
           ⎪ stitch <A row of weaving
           ⎱        <(D) buried row of weaving
turn reversal - - - - - - - - - - - - - - - - - - - - - - - - - - - - - -
           ⎰        B row of weaving
   4F      ⎪  long  C row of weaving
           ⎪ stitch <D row of weaving
           ⎱        <(A) half stitches
                Weaver
```

At this point, the next turn reversal should start, which will be a repeat of the four turns Backward.

After four cycles (4F / 4B / 4F / 4B), the band will look like this:

```
            long        long        long
             /\          /\          /\
Weaver    (A)DCB  /   (D)ABC  /   (A)DCB  /
             4F          4B          4F

                                     long
                                      /\
                                   (D)ABC      Cards
                                     4B
```

Omitting the turns which do not show on the surface of the weaving, would result in the following letter representation of the band:

```
                  *        *        *
Weaver     DCB  /  ABC  /  DCB  /  ABC     Cards
           4F       4B       4F      4B
```

Those letters with asterisks represent the long stitches. Removing the slashes, which represent the turn reversals, the draft would then show a print-out of the band as follows:

```
               *     *     *
Weaver     DCBABCDCBABC     Cards
```

Notice that each asterisk appears at a point where the letter it marks would have to appear *twice* if each cycle were to be complete with four letters from D to A and vice versa. Since each letter with the asterisk, is, in fact, the long stitch (covering a buried row of weaving), it is almost as if it *does appear twice* on the band:

DCBA / ABCD / DCBA / ABCD

It should be clear now how the warp ends get woven into a band in the order proceeding from the weaver to the cards. The draft is devised to represent the rows of weaving as they are completed when weaving Forward turns—if you hold the draft flat in front of you, the D row is closest to you, then the C row, the B row, and finally the A row farthest away—and that is exactly the order of the warp ends on the band in front of you as you are weaving. You should also be able to see why the mirror trick works. If the mirror is held along the top of the draft, the rows of weaving appear in reverse order—the A row, then the B row, the C row, and finally the D row—and that is the order they will appear on the band at the point of the turn reversal. The reflection shows the A row to be twice as long as the other rows. The turn reversal, because it buries another row of weaving, is twice as long as the other rows. Since it accounts for two rows of weaving, it is counted as two turns of the cards when making a tally of total turns (in the event that you lose your place, etc.) as advised in Chapter 4. Remember, also, that the angle of the stitch changes at the turn reversal (see Figure 4-26) and that generally accounts for heightened symmetry in a pattern.

The change in the slant of the stitches is also important to the overall pattern when adjacent cards are threaded in opposite directions. You undoubtedly remember from the Diagonal Experiment in Chapter 5 that cards threaded in opposite directions and turned in the same direction create stitches that slant in diverse directions. The changing angles of these stitches at a turn reversal are responsible for the two formations shown in Figure 4-26. When two stitches slant toward each other, they result in a little "Λ" shape after the turn is completed. A turn reversal prevents the convergence of these two stitches. They remain apart and, therefore, leave a little "hole" in the band through which the filling shows. Similarly, when two stitches slant away from each other, they form a "V" shape when the turn is completed. At the point of the reversal, the thrust of this outward motion is thwarted and the "V" shape cannot occur. The warp ends remain touching and, therefore, the center of the turn reversal appears to be a stitch of double thickness—or two stitches very close together, and in fact, practically on top of each other.

Knowing how these two reversal structures develop, should be of additional help when counting rows of weaving and mentally determining how a draft might look. This inherent feature of a reversal will not be apparent when using a mirror on a draft, because the draft (unlike the actual woven band) does not reproduce the slant of the stitches. It does, however, give an accurate color representation as well as a symmetric reflection of the pattern. The draft further shows the cards proceeding numerically from right to left as they are held when weaving.

If you now return to Pattern 40, you will perhaps better understand what happened there in order to achieve so many different patterns from one draft. Patterns 40A–C all offer the same Home Position, with different multiples of four as the cornerstones of the patterns. These should present no difficulty now that the mirror trick is clear; each one offers a longer section of the pattern before it reverses itself.

Patterns 40D–F all present new Home Positions. The reason why they each result in different designs (different from each other and from the basic printout of 40A–C) is that the turn reversal now occurs at a new point along the woven band. For example: Following the example of a standard band, which weaves out to DCBABCD, Pattern 40D weaves out to CBADABC, with the turn reversal occurring at C—with a longer stitch, of course. Pattern 40E gives BADCDAB and 40F gives ADCBCDA.

It should now be apparent why the pattern grids are set up as they are for drafting. When making your own drafts, it is practical to keep them uniform, in this style.

It is also a wise idea to keep a record of all your patterns—experiments and planned drafts alike. This can be done in the form of a pattern-draft book, similar in set-up to the workbook format of this volume. Be sure to include: number of cards, total number of warp ends (usually, but not always, this is four times the number of cards), warp breakdown by color, threading arrows, turning directions, and special instructions, where necessary. Instead of a photograph of the band, as is provided in this book, a sample of the finished piece can be included, if possible—a three-inch segment of the band is ideal to allow you to keep an accurate record of what the pattern looks like when woven.

ELABORATE PATTERNS

Following is a book of patterns of more elaborate, fancy designs than those presented in earlier chapters. Although photographs do not accompany every pattern, you should be able to mentally transpose the draft from paper to fiber without the aid of the photograph by tracing each color *through* the draft. These patterns can be woven in segments, as well. For example, border cards in one pattern may be transferred to another; smaller motifs in a pattern can be added as border cards to another pattern, etc., thus creating new patterns. Many, many more designs can be created from these drafts by changing color schemes. Of course, the combinations are endless.

There is a good way to test different colors and disparately textured fibers for compatability in a woven band. This is done by taking together a length (about ten to twelve inches is sufficient) of each proposed fiber. Hold all of them in one hand and with the other hand twirl them around so they twist over one another. This is a fairly accurate way to determine how they will look when woven into a tight band. (Remember, card weaving is really a twisting of the warp ends.) It is a good practice to always do this color test before weaving; it is not unusual to be misled into thinking that certain colors will look well together when viewed on skeins or spools, only to discover when weaving that the combination is disastrous. This is particularly true of pastel shades, which generally lack the vibrant quality necessary in card weaving to distinguish a design.

Pattern 44

Warp Fiber: Orlon
Filling Fiber: Same as warp
Warp Ends: 40
Warp Breakdown: 24 Blue
                        16 White
Turning: All Forward

This band can be seen in Color Plate C-8 as the shoulder strap of a small woven tote. Notice that two of the colors from the bag—the blue and the white—were carried through to the strap.

10	9	8	7	6	5	4	3	2	1	
B	B	W	W	W	B	B	W	B	B	A
B	B	W	B	B	W	W	W	B	B	B
B	B	W	W	W	B	B	W	B	B	C
B	B	W	B	B	W	W	W	B	B	D
↖	↖	↖	↖	↖	↖	↖	↖	↖	↖	

9-1. Draft for Pattern 44.

Pattern 45

Warp Fiber: Cotton
Filling Fiber: Same as warp
Warp Ends: 92
Warp Breakdown: 42 Blue
                        28 Green
                        22 Yellow
Turning: 4F / 4B

Pattern 46

Warp Fiber: Tubular velvet
Filling Fiber: Thin Orlon (white)
Warp Ends: 36
Warp Breakdown: 18 White
                        9 Red
                        9 Blue
Turning: 4F / 4B

See this pattern in Color Plate C-3 as the strap of a pocketbook. Woven from tubular velvet, this pattern is particularly rich and thick. For best results, weave with a very heavy fiber (such as the velvet used here) as warp and a thin fiber as filling. Had tubular velvet been used for the filling as well as the warp, this band would have been much too thick to use. As it is, it is perfect for its function.

9	8	7	6	5	4	3	2	1	
W	R	B	B	B	B	B	R	W	A
R	W	R	B	B	B	R	W	R	B
W	W	W	R	B	R	W	W	W	C
W	W	W	W	R	W	W	W	W	D
↖	↖	↖	↖	↗	↗	↗	↗	↗	

9-3. Draft for Pattern 46.

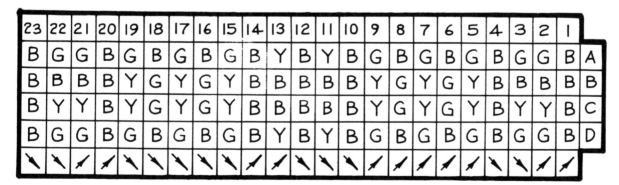

23	22	21	20	19	18	17	16	15	14	13	12	11	10	9	8	7	6	5	4	3	2	1	
B	G	G	B	G	B	G	B	G	B	Y	B	Y	B	G	B	G	B	G	B	G	G	B	A
B	B	B	B	Y	G	Y	G	Y	B	B	B	B	B	Y	G	Y	G	Y	B	B	B	B	B
B	Y	Y	B	Y	G	Y	G	Y	B	B	B	B	B	Y	G	Y	G	Y	B	Y	Y	B	C
B	G	G	B	G	B	G	B	G	B	Y	B	Y	B	G	B	G	B	G	B	G	G	B	D
↖	↖	↗	↗	↖	↗	↖	↗	↖	↖	↖	↖	↖	↖	↗	↗	↗	↗	↗	↖	↖	↗	↗	

9-2. Draft for Pattern 45.

Pattern 47

Warp Fiber: Cordé
Filling Fiber: Same as warp (black)
Warp Ends: 76
Warp Breakdown: 29 Black
                         29 White
                         18 Gray
Turning: 4F / 4B

Both sides of this band are interesting and different. Color Plate C-14 illustrates how attractive this belt looks with a silver buckle.

Pattern 48

Warp Fiber: Thin-gauge rattail
Filling Fiber: Same as warp (beige)
Warp Ends: 64
Warp Breakdown: 24 Beige
                         18 Loden green
                         12 Gold
                         10 Rust
Turning: 4F / 4B

This pattern is illustrated in Color Plate C-11.

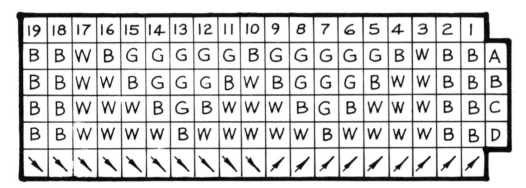

19	18	17	16	15	14	13	12	11	10	9	8	7	6	5	4	3	2	1	
B	B	W	B	G	G	G	G	B	G	G	G	G	B	W	B	B	A
B	B	W	W	B	G	G	G	B	W	B	G	G	G	B	W	W	B	B	B
B	B	W	W	W	B	G	B	W	W	W	B	G	B	W	W	W	B	B	C
B	B	W	W	W	W	B	W	W	W	W	W	B	W	W	W	W	B	B	D

9-4a, b, c. Draft and front and back of band, Pattern 47.

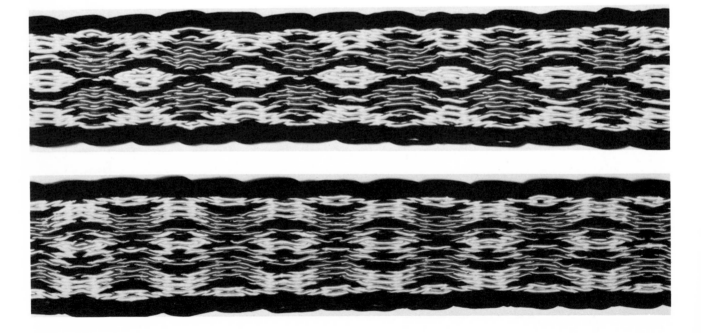

116

16	15	14	13	12	11	10	9	8	7	6	5	4	3	2	1	
B	R	B	R	L	R	B	G	G	B	R	L	R	B	R	B	A
B	L	L	B	R	B	G	R	R	G	B	R	B	L	L	B	B
B	B	L	L	B	G	L	L	L	L	G	B	G	L	B	B	C
B	L	B	G	G	B	L	G	G	L	B	G	L	B	L	B	D

9-5. Draft for Pattern 48.

Pattern 49

Warp Fiber: Crinkle cord
Filling Fiber: Same as warp (blue)
Warp Ends: 52
Warp Breakdown: 20 Blue
                       17 Purple
                       15 Green
Turning: 4F / 4B

This band is also shown in Color Plate C-13. Both this pattern and Pattern 50 can be changed greatly by transposing the threading directions of each half of the bands.

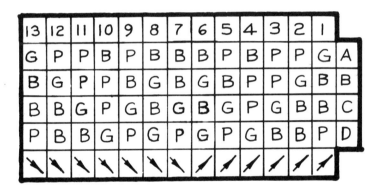

13	12	11	10	9	8	7	6	5	4	3	2	1	
G	P	P	B	P	B	B	B	P	B	P	P	G	A
B	G	P	P	B	G	B	G	B	P	P	G	B	B
B	B	G	P	G	B	G	B	G	P	G	B	B	C
P	B	B	G	P	G	P	G	P	G	B	B	P	D

9-6a, b. Draft and band, Pattern 49.

Pattern 50

Warp Fiber: Thin-gauge rattail
Filling Fiber: Same as warp (blue)
Warp Ends: 52
Warp Breakdown: 24 White
19 Red
9 Blue

Turning: 8F / 8B

Figure 4-24 shows how this pattern looks, worked in the same colors used in Pattern 51, when a single card becomes unaligned. This band is illustrated in Color Plate C-6.

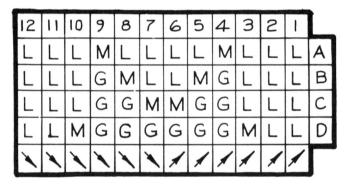

13	12	11	10	9	8	7	6	5	4	3	2	1	
R	W	W	R	B	B	B	B	B	R	W	W	R	A
R	W	R	W	R	B	B	B	R	W	R	W	R	B
R	R	W	W	R	B	R	W	W	W	R	R		C
R	W	W	W	W	W	R	W	W	W	W	R		D
↘	↘	↘	↘	↘	↘	↘	↗	↗	↗	↗	↗	↗	

9-7. Draft for Pattern 50.

Pattern 51

Warp Fiber: Thin-gauge rattail
Filling Fiber: Same as warp (lilac)
Warp Ends: 48
Warp Breakdown: 28 Lilac
12 Loden Green
8 Maroon

Turning: 8F / 8B

Notice how startlingly different the two sides of this band are. The print is very reminiscent of Indian patterns (as is Pattern 47) and, is enhanced by the style of buckle, shown in Color Plate C-14, which underscores its symmetry.

12	11	10	9	8	7	6	5	4	3	2	1	
L	L	L	M	L	L	L	M	L	L	L		A
L	L	L	G	M	L	L	M	G	L	L	L	B
L	L	L	G	G	M	M	G	G	L	L	L	C
L	L	M	G	G	G	G	G	M	L	L		D
↘	↘	↘	↘	↘	↘	↗	↗	↗	↗	↗	↗	

9-8a, b. Draft, front and back of band, Pattern 51.

Pattern 52

Warp Fiber: Crinkle cord
Filling Fiber: Same as warp (red)
Warp Ends: 44
Warp Breakdown: 16 Red
  15 White
  13 Black
Turning: 2F / 2B / 2F / 2B / 2F / 2B / 1F / 1B / repeat

This band is illustrated in Color Plate C-13.

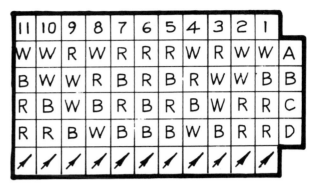

9-9. Draft for Pattern 52.

Pattern 53

Warp Fiber: Thin-gauge rattail
Filling Fiber: same as warp (blue)
Warp Ends: 28
Warp Breakdown: 12 Blue
  9 Lilac
  7 Purple
Turning: 4F / 4B

This band is illustrated in Color Plate C-15.

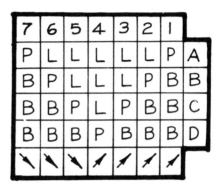

9-10. Draft for Pattern 53.

Pattern 54

Warp Fiber: Heavy-gauge rattail
Filling Fiber: Thin-gauge rattail (royal blue)
Warp Ends: 52
Warp Breakdown: 19 Royal Blue
  11 Kelly Green
  11 Light Blue
  11 Gold
Turning: 8F / 8B

This band is shown in Color Plate C-11.

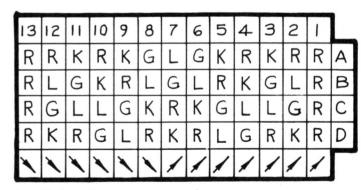

9-11. Draft for Pattern 54.

Pattern 55

Warp Fiber: Chainnette
Filling Fiber: Same as warp (canary)
Warp Ends: 84
Warp Breakdown: 56 Canary
                     14 Magenta
                     14 Peach
Turning: 12F / 12B

This draft is asymmetric, but the pattern doesn't have a lopsided look, despite that fact.

Pattern 56

Warp Fiber: Thin-gauge rattail
Filling Fiber: Same as warp (navy blue)
Warp Ends: 72
Warp Breakdown: 18 Rust
                     18 Navy Blue
                     18 Peach
                     18 Beige
Turning: 4F / 4B

This pattern is illustrated in Color Plate C-15.

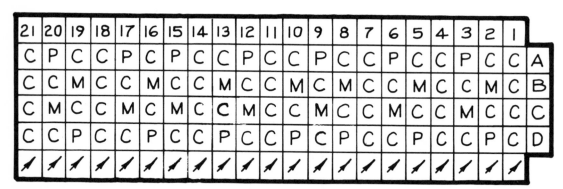

21	20	19	18	17	16	15	14	13	12	11	10	9	8	7	6	5	4	3	2	1	
C	P	C	C	P	C	P	C	C	P	C	C	P	C	C	P	C	C	P	C	C	A
C	C	M	C	C	M	C	C	M	C	C	M	C	M	C	C	M	C	C	M	C	B
C	M	C	C	M	C	M	C	C	M	C	C	M	C	C	M	C	C	M	C	C	C
C	C	P	C	C	P	C	C	P	C	C	P	C	P	C	C	P	C	C	P	C	D

9-12a, b. Draft and band, Pattern 55.

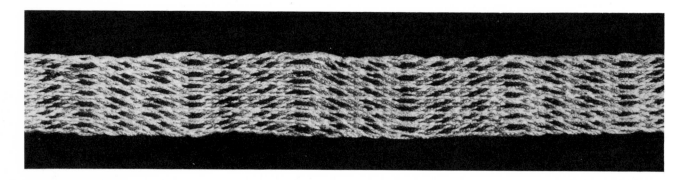

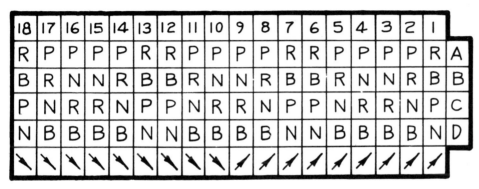

18	17	16	15	14	13	12	11	10	9	8	7	6	5	4	3	2	1	
R	P	P	P	P	R	R	P	P	P	P	R	R	P	P	P	P	R	A
B	R	N	N	R	B	B	R	N	N	R	B	B	R	N	N	R	B	B
P	N	R	R	N	P	P	N	R	R	N	P	P	N	R	R	N	P	C
N	B	B	B	B	N	N	B	B	B	B	N	N	B	B	B	B	N	D
↘	↘	↘	↘	↘	↘	↘	↘	↘	↘	↗	↗	↗	↗	↗	↗	↗	↗	

9-13. Draft for Pattern 56.

Pattern 57

Warp Fiber: Linen and perlé
Filling Fiber: Perlé (turquoise and brown)
Warp Ends: 68
Warp Breakdown: 52 Natural Linen
                         12 Turquoise Perlé
                          4 Brown Perlé

Turning: 8F / 8B

This belt was woven with a dowel attached to the right-hand selvage of the weaving to make turquoise and brown fringe. This fringing technique is explained in Chapter 7. The field is natural linen, the pattern turquoise and brown perlé.

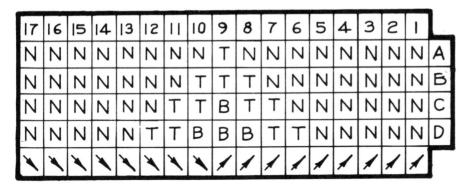

17	16	15	14	13	12	11	10	9	8	7	6	5	4	3	2	1	
N	N	N	N	N	N	N	T	N	N	N	N	N	N	N	N	N	A
N	N	N	N	N	N	T	T	T	N	N	N	N	N	N	N	N	B
N	N	N	N	N	T	T	B	T	T	N	N	N	N	N	N	N	C
N	N	N	N	T	T	B	B	B	T	T	N	N	N	N	N	N	D
↘	↘	↘	↘	↘	↘	↘	↘	↗	↗	↗	↗	↗	↗	↗	↗	↗	

9-14a, b. Draft and band, Pattern 57.

Pattern 58

Warp Fiber: Line braid
Filling Fiber: Same as warp (red)
Warp Ends: 112
Warp Breakdown: 40 White
                       40 Blue
                       32 Red

Turning: 4F / 4B

9-15. Draft for Pattern 58.

25	24	23	22	21	20	19	18	17	16	15	14	13	12	11	10	9	8	7	6	5	4	3	2	1	
R	R	W	W	B	B	B	W	W	B	B	B	B	W	W	B	B	B	W	W	R	R	B	W	R	A
R	R	W	W	B	B	R	W	W	R	W	W	R	W	W	R	B	B	W	W	R	R	B	W	R	B
R	R	W	W	B	B	R	B	B	R	W	W	R	B	B	R	B	B	W	W	R	R	B	W	R	C
R	R	W	W	B	B	B	W	W	B	B	B	B	W	W	B	B	B	W	W	R	R	B	W	R	D

9-16. Draft for Pattern 59.

28	27	26	
R	W	B	A
R	W	B	B
R	W	B	C
R	W	B	D

Pattern 59

Warp Fiber: 6/3 twist
Filling Fiber: Same as warp (blue)
Warp Ends: 96
Warp Breakdown: 44 Blue
                       28 Green
                       24 Red

Turning: 8F / 8B

The close-up color detail of this pattern, Color Plate C-12, emphasizes the delicate nature of the 6/3 twist fiber, as well as its gloss and vibrant color. It is ideal for trim for uniforms where it can be worked in with gold braiding.

24	23	22	21	20	19	18	17	16	15	14	13	12	11	10	9	8	7	6	5	4	3	2	1	
B	B	B	B	B	B	R	B	B	B	G	G	B	B	B	R	R	B	B	B	B	B	B	A
B	B	G	G	G	R	R	G	G	G	G	R	R	R	G	G	G	G	B	B	B			B
B	B	G	G	G	R	R	G	G	G	R	R	R	R	G	G	G	B	B	C				C
B	B	B	B	B	B	R	R	B	B	B	G	B	B	B	R	R	B	B	B	B	B	B	D

122

Patterns 60, 61, and 62

Warp Fiber: Needlepoint wool
Filling Fiber: Same (red)
Warp Ends: 96
Warp Breakdown: 48 Red
                      24 Black
                      24 White
Turning: Pattern 60, 4F / 4B
          Pattern 61, 8F / 8B
          Pattern 62, 12F / 12B / 2F / 2B / repeat

Notice that these three patterns all have the same numerical distribution of warp ends (48 red, 24 black, and 24 white), although their arrangement is slightly different in each. The direction of the threading of the cards is the same for all three patterns, but each set of turning instructions is different. This was a highly successful exercise/experiment, and if you take the time to do these three patterns, you will find the results (various circles and diamond shapes) interesting.

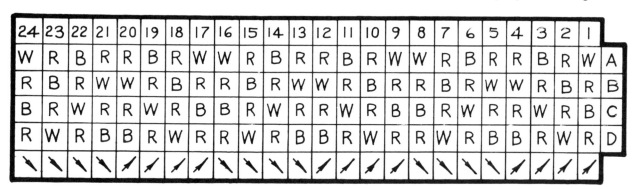

9-17. Draft for Pattern 60.

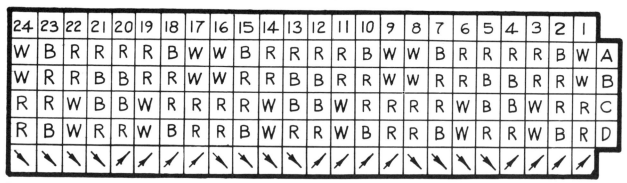

9-18. Draft for Pattern 61

24	23	22	21	20	19	18	17	16	15	14	13	12	11	10	9	8	7	6	5	4	3	2	1	
W	R	B	R	R	B	R	W	W	R	B	R	R	B	R	W	W	R	B	R	R	B	R	W	A
R	W	R	B	B	R	W	R	R	W	R	B	B	R	W	R	R	W	R	B	B	R	W	R	B
B	R	W	R	R	W	R	B	B	R	W	R	R	W	R	B	B	R	W	R	R	W	R	B	C
R	B	R	W	W	R	B	R	R	B	R	W	W	R	B	R	R	B	R	W	W	R	B	R	D

9-19. Draft for Pattern 62.

Pattern 63

Warp Fiber: 6/3 twist
Filling Fiber: Same as warp (red)
Warp Ends: 160
Warp Breakdown: 88 Red
                              44 White
                              28 Blue

Turning: 4F / 4B

Notice the braiding effect of this pattern, shown in Color Plate C-21. Because the draft has "blocks" of patterns within the structure of the major, over-all pattern, it is ideal for this sort of plaiting, as described in Chapter 7. The other side of the band is also very attractive and it was difficult to decide which side to use on the show side.

Pattern 64

Warp Fiber: Chainnette
Filling Fiber: Same as warp (black)
Warp Ends: 208
Warp Breakdown: 70 Black
                              32 Pink
                              24 Magenta
                              22 Green
                              22 Light Blue
                              20 Coral
                              18 Yellow

Turning: 8F / 8B

This pattern is also ideal (as is Pattern 63) for plaiting segments of the band—particularly because of the definitive, black-edged borders. The gay colors of this belt make a black dress absolutely dazzling!

9-20. Draft for Pattern 63.

25	24	23	22	21	20	19	18	17	16	15	14	13	12	11	10	9	8	7	6	5	4	3	2	1	
W	W	W	B	B	B	B	W	W	W	R	R	R	R	B	W	B	W	B	R	R	R	R	R	R	A
W	W	B	W	B	B	W	B	W	W	R	R	R	R	W	R	W	R	W	R	R	R	R	R	R	B
W	B	W	W	B	B	W	W	B	W	R	R	R	R	W	R	W	R	W	R	R	R	R	R	R	C
B	W	W	W	B	B	W	W	W	B	R	R	R	R	B	W	B	W	B	R	R	R	R	R	R	D

40	39	38	37	36	35	34	33	32	31	30	29	28	27	26	
R	R	R	R	R	B	W	B	W	B	R	R	R	R	R	A
R	R	R	R	R	W	R	W	R	W	R	R	R	R	R	B
R	R	R	R	R	W	R	W	R	W	R	R	R	R	R	C
R	R	R	R	R	B	W	B	W	B	R	R	R	R	R	D

25	24	23	22	21	20	19	18	17	16	15	14	13	12	11	10	9	8	7	6	5	4	3	2	1	
P	G	Y	B	Y	G	P	L	L	C	L	L	B	B	B	B	P	G	P	G	P	B	B	B	B	A
M	P	G	Y	G	P	M	L	C	C	C	L	B	B	B	B	Y	P	G	P	Y	B	B	B	B	B
M	M	P	G	P	M	M	C	C	C	C	C	B	B	B	B	P	Y	P	Y	P	B	B	B	B	C
M	M	M	P	M	M	M	L	L	L	L	L	B	B	B	B	Y	G	G	G	Y	B	B	B	B	D
↘	↘	↘	↗	↗	↗	↗	↘	↗	↗	↘	↗	↘	↗	↘	↗	↘	↗	↗	↗	↗	↘	↘	↗	↗	

9-21. Draft for Pattern 64.

50	49	48	47	46	45	44	43	42	41	40	39	38	37	36	35	34	33	32	31	30	29	28	27	26	
B	B	P	G	P	G	P	B	B	B	B	L	L	C	L	L	P	G	Y	B	Y	G	P	B	B	A
B	B	Y	P	G	P	Y	B	B	B	B	L	C	C	C	L	M	P	G	Y	G	P	M	Y	Y	B
B	B	P	Y	P	Y	P	B	B	B	B	C	C	C	C	C	M	M	P	G	P	M	M	P	P	C
B	B	Y	G	G	G	Y	B	B	B	B	L	L	L	L	L	M	M	M	P	M	M	M	C	C	D
↗	↗	↘	↘	↘	↗	↗	↘	↘	↗	↗	↘	↗	↘	↗	↘	↗	↗	↘	↘	↘	↗	↗	↗	↗	

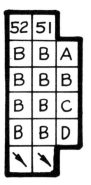

52	51	
B	B	A
B	B	B
B	B	C
B	B	D
↘	↘	

The following eleven drafts are all based on chevron or step motifs and are, therefore, similar to early Egyptian patterns. Each is marked by striking symmetry in the overall design as well as in the internal arrangements of the minimotifs within the framework of the whole band. This entire group should be rendered with very bold colors. Experiment with various turning sequences and plaiting techniques, as these patterns lend themselves well to both.

None of these eleven patterns is presented in photographs, so allow your imagination to run wild in selection of color! The keys for the warp breakdowns are all presented in terms of symbols. Note: A plain white box on these drafts does not indicate the omission technique of the Swedish weaves, but rather is representative of a color group of warp ends. Unless otherwise noted, all four holes in each card are threaded. As in all the other patterns in this workbook section, there is adequate room to insert the colors which the reader chooses to use.

Pattern 65

Warp Ends: 196
Warp Breakdown: 73 = ■
  67 = X
  56 = □

9-22. Draft for pattern 65.

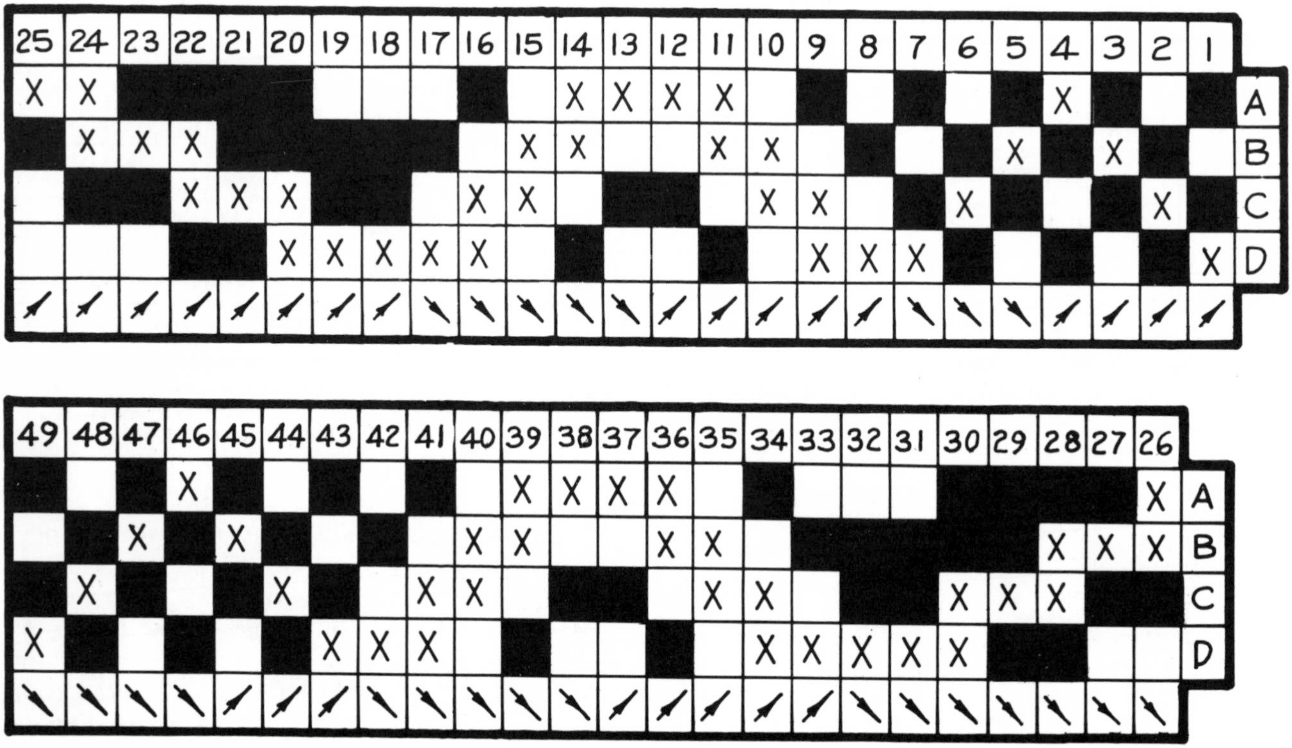

25	24	23	22	21	20	19	18	17	16	15	14	13	12	11	10	9	8	7	6	5	4	3	2	1	
X	X		■	■				■		■	X	X	X	X		■		■		■	X	■	■	■	A
■	X	X	X						■	X	X			■	X	X		■		X		X	■		B
	■		X	X	X	■			X	X		■			X	X		■	X		■		X		C
			■	X	X	X	X	X			■			■		X	X	X	■					X	D
✓	✓	✓	✓	✓	✓	✓	✓	✓	✓	✓	✓	✓	✓	✓	✓	✓	✓	✓	✓	✓	✓	✓	✓	✓	

49	48	47	46	45	44	43	42	41	40	39	38	37	36	35	34	33	32	31	30	29	28	27	26	
■		■	X			■				X	X	X	X	■				■					X	A
■		X	■	X		■		X	X			X	X		■						X	X	X	B
	X	■		■	X	X		■			X	X		■				X	X	X	■			C
X	■		■		X	X	X			■		■		X	X	X	X	X	■					D
✓	✓	✓	✓	✓	✓	✓	✓	✓	✓	✓	✓	✓	✓	✓	✓	✓	✓	✓	✓	✓	✓	✓	✓	

126

Pattern 66

Warp Ends: 216

Warp Breakdown:
- 86 = █
- 48 = X
- 46 = 0
- 36 = (blank)

9-23. Draft for Pattern 66.

25	24	23	22	21	20	19	18	17	16	15	14	13	12	11	10	9	8	7	6	5	4	3	2	1	
		█	█	█	X	X	█	X	X	█	█	█		█	█	█	X	X	█	X	X	█	█	█	A
		X	█	█	█	X	█	X	█	█	X	█	X	█	█	█	X	█	X	█	█	█	X		B
█		X	X	█	█	█	█	█	█	█	X	X	█	X	X	█	█	█	█	█	█	X	X	█	C
		0	0	0	0	0		0	0	0	0	0		0	0	0	0	0		0	0	0	0	0	D
↗	↘	↗	↘	↗	↘	↗	↘	↗	↘	↗	↘	↗	↘	↗	↘	↗	↘	↗	↘	↗	↘	↗	↘	↗	

50	49	48	47	46	45	44	43	42	41	40	39	38	37	36	35	34	33	32	31	30	29	28	27	26	
X		X	X	█	█	█		█	█	█	X	X	█	X	X	█	█	█				█	█	█	A
X		X	█	█	X	█	█	X	█	█	X	█	X	█	█	X	█	X	█	█	█				B
			X	X	█	█	X	X	█	█	█	█	█	█	█	█	X	X	█	█	0	0	█	█	C
0		0	0	0	0	0		0	0	0	0	0		0	0	0	0	0	█	0	0	0	0	0	D
↗	↘	↗	↘	↗	↘	↗	↘	↗	↘	↗	↘	↗	↘	↗	↘	↗	↘	↗	↘	↗	↘	↗	↘	↗	

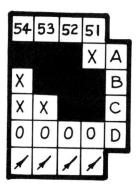

54	53	52	51	
█	█	█	X	A
X	█	█	█	B
X	X	█	█	C
0	0	0	0	D
↗	↘	↗	↘	

Pattern 67

Warp Ends: 220

Warp Breakdown: 56 = ⊠

56 = ⊡

54 = ☐ (white)

54 = ■ (black)

9-24. Draft for Pattern 67.

25	24	23	22	21	20	19	18	17	16	15	14	13	12	11	10	9	8	7	6	5	4	3	2	1	
0				0	X	■	■	■	X	0				0	X	■	■	■	X	■					A
0	0	0	0	0	X	X	X	X	X	0	0	0	0	0	X	X	X	X	X	■	■				B
X	X	X	X	X	0	0	0	0	0	X	X	X	X	X	0	0	0	0	0	■	■	■			C
X	■	■	■		X	0			0	X	■	■	■		X	0			0	■	■	■	■		D
↘	↘	↘	↘	↘	↗	↗	↗	↗	↗	↘	↘	↘	↘	↘	↗	↗	↗	↗	↗	↗	↗	↗	↗	↗	

50	49	48	47	46	45	44	43	42	41	40	39	38	37	36	35	34	33	32	31	30	29	28	27	26	
X	■	■	■		X	0			0	X	■	■	■		X	0			0	■				■	A
X	X	X	X	X	0	0	0	0	0	X	X	X	X	X	0	0	0	0	0		■		■		B
0	0	0	0	0	X	X	X	X	X	0	0	0	0	0	X	X	X	X	X		■		■		C
0				0	X	■	■	■	X	0				0	X	■	■	■	X	■				■	D
↘	↘	↘	↘	↘	↗	↗	↗	↗	↗	↘	↘	↘	↘	↘	↗	↗	↗	↗	↗	↗	↘	↗	↗	↗	

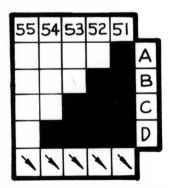

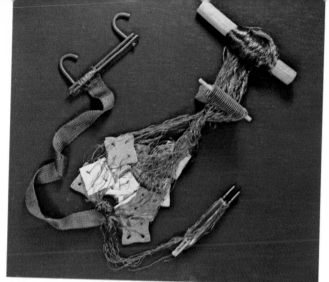

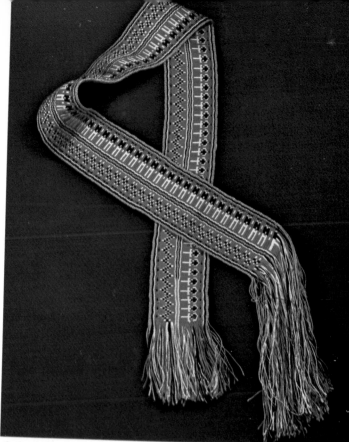

C-2.
C-4.

C-1.
C-3.

C-1. Delachaux, a colleague of Van Gennep and Jéquier, became so fascinated with the controversy over the Girdle of Rameses III that he tried his hand at reconstructing a segment. This section of his card-woven band is reproduced in its proper colors and features the "ankh" motif. (Musée d'Ethnographie, Neuchâtel)

C-2. A loom for card weaving with wooden appointments, including a comb. This loom may have been brought back from Algeria by Van Gennep during the course of his research. (Musée d'Ethnographie, Neuchatel)

C-3. A pocketbook woven out of heavy, tubular velvet. The strap is made from Pattern 46.

C-4. A band brought back from Algeria by Van Gennep, 1913. (Musée d'Ethnographie, Neuchâtel)

C-5.
C-6.

C-7.
C-8.

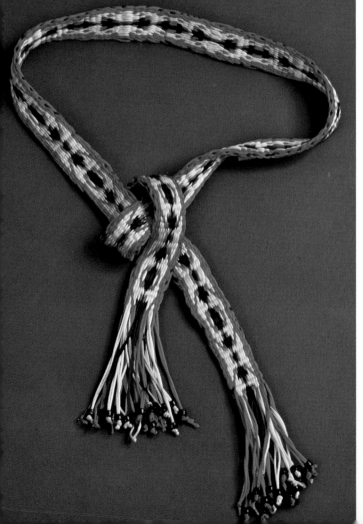

C-10.
C-9.

C-5. A gaily colored belt with a buckle that compliments it perfectly. Notice the stitched and fringed end.

C-6. A belt woven from Pattern 50. Notice the navy blue filling that appears regularly along the edges.

C-7. Pattern 10, a simple stripe, becomes quite dazzling with both ends completed with beads and macramé.

C-8. The color-coordinated strap for this bag was woven from Pattern 44.

C-9. Left, Pattern 22; middle, Pattern 16; right, Pattern 23.

C-10. Leftover Christmas gift-wrap tie was used to weave Pattern 20; the result is a very sturdy and elegant handle for this dressy pocketbook.

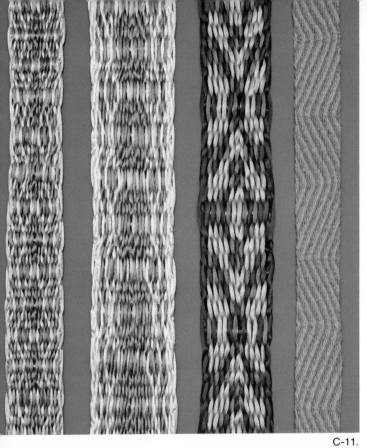

C-11.   C-13.

C-12.   C-15.

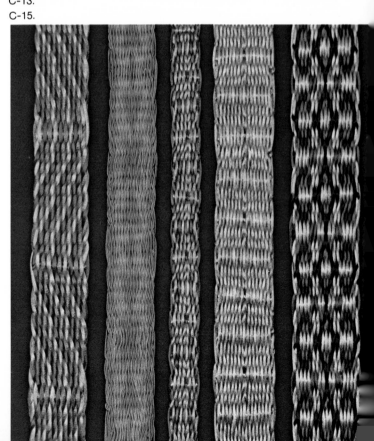

C-14.

C-11. Four bands, from left to right: Pattern 48, an experimental band, Pattern 54, and Pattern 29.

C-12. Right, a band woven from Pattern 59 without filling. Left, the same band woven with filling. The pattern on the right without the filling emerges with even edges and an indistinct design.

C-13. Fringed ends, finished in several different ways: left, Pattern 49; middle, a pattern similar to 36 but woven with turn reversals; and right, Pattern 52.

C-14. Choosing a belt buckle should be done with the style of the belt and its purpose in mind: from top to bottom: Pattern 51; Patterns 6 and 21; Pattern 47; (fourth row not given in patterns.); and Pattern 33.

C-15. Contrasting colors work best for card weaving. The pastel shades of the three center bands do not show the patterns distinctly. From left to right: Pattern 28; a pattern similar to 50; Pattern 53; an experimental band to show pastel colors; Pattern 56.

133

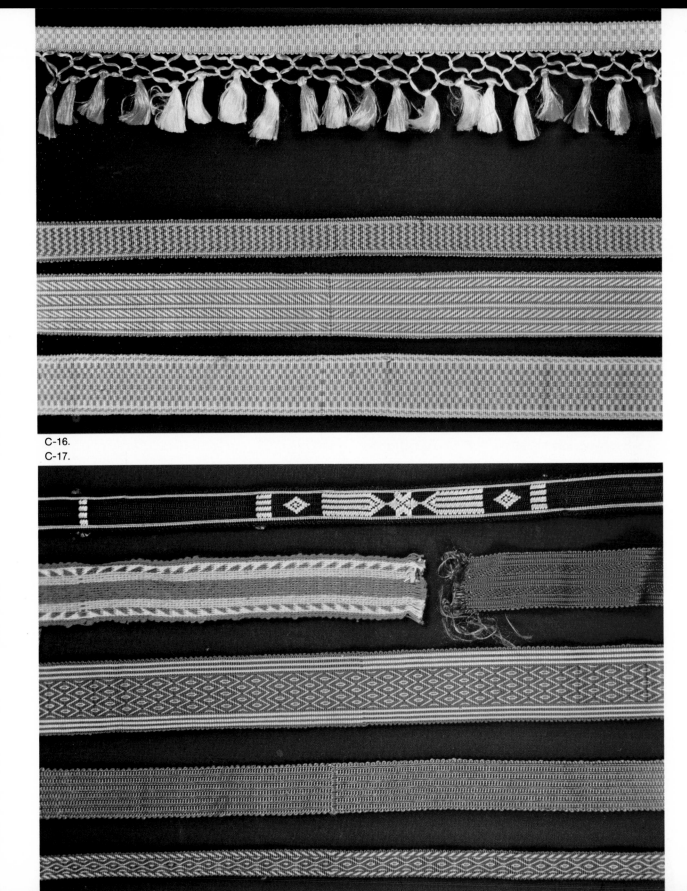

C-16.
C-17.

C-19.
C-18.

C-16. Card-woven bands probably from Algeria. The tassels on the top example change the total look of the band. (Musée d'Ethnographie, Neuchâtel)

C-17. Card-woven bands probably from Algeria. (Musée d'Ethnographie, Neuchâtel)

C-18. A solid pattern woven out of white double-faced satin ribbon (Pattern 4). The completed band, threaded through a chain-link belt makes a very attractive belt.

C-19. A white card-woven band with buttonholes for a plain wool sweater. The band is a combination of silk and rayon.

C-20.
C-21.

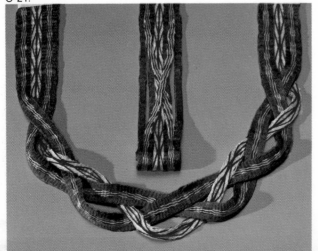

C-20. A plain black sweater is transformed into quite an original design with a little embroidery and a color-coordinated band, woven from Pattern 23, across the bottom edge.

C-21. These two bands, woven from Pattern 63 show examples of criss-crossing segments of a band that are composed of small motifs. The larger piece, when lying flat, is a large braid; as shown here, it is ideal for a neck piece.

Pattern 68

Warp Ends: 196

Warp Breakdown: 92 = ■

52 = X

28 = □

24 = 0

9-25. Draft for Pattern 68.

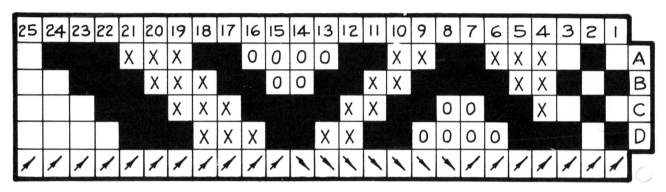

137

Pattern 69
Warp Ends: 216
Warp Breakdown: 60 = X
60 = 0
56 = ☐
40 = ■

9-26. Draft for pattern 69.

25	24	23	22	21	20	19	18	17	16	15	14	13	12	11	10	9	8	7	6	5	4	3	2	1	
X	X			█	█	█	█	█	█	█	█			X	X	X	O	O	X	X	X				A
X	X			X	█	█	█	█	█		X			X	X	O	O	O	O	X	X				B
O	X			X	X	█	█	█	█	X	X			X	O	O	O	O	O	O	X				C
O				X	X	X	█	█	X	X	X			O	O	O	O	O	O	O	O				D
↙	↙	↙	↙	↙	↙	↙	↙	↙	↙	↙	↙	↙	↙	↙	↙	↙	↙	↙	↙	↙	↙	↙	↙	↙	

50	49	48	47	46	45	44	43	42	41	40	39	38	37	36	35	34	33	32	31	30	29	28	27	26	
X	X	O	O	X	X	X			█	█	█	█	█	█	█	█			X	X	X	O	O	X	A
X	O	O	O	X	X				X	█	█	█	█	█	█	X			X	X	O	O	O	O	B
O	O	O	O	O	X				X	X	█	█	█	█	X	X			X	O	O	O	O	O	C
O	O	O	O	O					X	X	X	█	█	X	X	X			O	O	O	O	O	O	D
↙	↙	↙	↙	↙	↙	↙	↙	↙	↙	↙	↙	↙	↙	↙	↙	↙	↙	↙	↙	↙	↙	↙	↙	↙	

54	53	52	51	
			X	A
			X	B
			X	C
			O	D
↙	↙	↙	↙	

138

Pattern 70

Warp Ends: 220

Warp Breakdown:
60 =	X
56 =	O
40 =	△
32 =	■
32 =	□

9-27. Draft for Pattern 70.

25	24	23	22	21	20	19	18	17	16	15	14	13	12	11	10	9	8	7	6	5	4	3	2	1	
					X	X	X	X	O	O	■	■	■	O	O	X	X	O	O	■	■	■	O	O	A
△		X	X	X	X	■	■		△	△	O	O	O	△	△	X	X	△	△	O	O	O	△	△	B
	X	X	X	X	■	■	△		△	△	O	O	O	△	△	X	X	△	△	O	O	O	△	△	C
X	X	X	■	■	■	■	■	△	O	O				O	O	X	X	O	O				O	O	D
↙	↙	↘	↙	↙	↙	↙	↘	↙	↙	↘	↙	↙	↙	↘	↘	↘	↙	↘	↙	↙	↘	↙	↘	↙	

50	49	48	47	46	45	44	43	42	41	40	39	38	37	36	35	34	33	32	31	30	29	28	27	26	
O	O	X	X	O	O	■	■	■	O	O	X	X	X	X						△	X	X	X	△	A
△	△	X	X	△	△	O	O	O	△	△	■			X	X	X	X		△		X	X	X		B
△	△	X	X	△	△	O	O	O	△	△	■	△	■	■	X	X	X	X			X	X	X		C
O	O	X	X	O	O				O	O	△	■	■	■	■	X	X	X	X	X	X	X	X	X	D
↙	↘	↙	↙	↘	↙	↙	↙	↙	↙	↙	↙	↙	↙	↙	↙	↙	↙	↙	↙	↙	↙	↙	↘	↘	

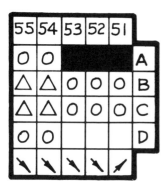

55	54	53	52	51	
O	O	■	■	■	A
△	△	O	O	O	B
△	△	O	O	O	C
O	O				D
↘	↘	↘	↘	↙	

Pattern 71

Warp Ends: 192

Warp Breakdown: 90 = X
54 = O
48 = ☐

9-28. Draft for Pattern 71.

25	24	23	22	21	20	19	18	17	16	15	14	13	12	11	10	9	8	7	6	5	4	3	2	1	
X	X	X	X	X	X				X	X	O	O	O	O	O	X	X	X			X	X	X		A
O	O	X	X	X			X	X		X	O	X	X	X	X	X	X		X	X			X	X	B
O	O	X	X		O	X	X	O			X	X	X	X	O	X		O	O	O	O			X	C
X	X	X			X	O	O	O	O	X			O	O	O	O		X	O	O	O	O	X		D

48	47	46	45	44	43	42	41	40	39	38	37	36	35	34	33	32	31	30	29	28	27	26	
X	X	X		X	X	X	O	O	O	O	O	X	X						X	X	X	X	A
X	X		X	X		X	X	X	X	X	X	O	X			X	X			X	X	X	B
X		O	O	O	O		X	O	X	X	X			O	X	X	O			X	X		C
X	O	O	O	O	X		O	O	O	O		X	O	O	O	O	X				X		D

140

Pattern 72

Warp Ends: 176

Warp Breakdown: 62 = ☒ (X)
60 = ☐
54 = Ⓞ (0)

9-29. Draft for pattern 72.

25	24	23	22	21	20	19	18	17	16	15	14	13	12	11	10	9	8	7	6	5	4	3	2	1	
		O	O									O	O								X	X	X	X	A
O	O	O	O	O	O					O	O	O	O	O	O						X	X	X	X	B
O	O	O	O	O	O	O	O	O	O	O	O	O	O	O	O	O					X	X	X	X	C
X	X	X	X	X	X	X	X	X	X	X	X	X	X	X	X	X					X	X	X	X	D

44	43	42	41	40	39	38	37	36	35	34	33	32	31	30	29	28	27	26	
X	X	X	X								O	O							A
X	X	X	X						O	O	O	O	O	O					B
X	X	X	X				O	O	O	O	O	O	O	O	O	O	O	O	C
X	X	X	X				X	X	X	X	X	X	X	X	X	X	X	X	D

141

Pattern 73

Warp Ends: 208

Warp Breakdown: 92 = ☐
      60 = X
      56 = 0

9-30. Draft for pattern 73.

25	24	23	22	21	20	19	18	17	16	15	14	13	12	11	10	9	8	7	6	5	4	3	2	1	
		X	X	X	X	X	0			0	X	X	X	X	X			0	0	X	X		0	X	A
		X	X	0	X	0				0	X	0	X	X				0	0	X	X		0	X	B
		X	0		0					0		0		0				0	0	X	X		0	X	C
		0													0			0	0	X	X		0	X	D
↗	↗	↘	↗	↘	↗	↘	↗	↘	↗	↗	↗	↗	↗	↗	↘	↗	↘	↗	↘	↗	↘	↗	↗	↗	

50	49	48	47	46	45	44	43	42	41	40	39	38	37	36	35	34	33	32	31	30	29	28	27	26	
	X	X	0	0			X	X	X	X	X	0			0	X	X	X	X	X			0	0	A
	X	X	0	0			X	X	0	X	0				0	X	0	X	X				0	0	B
	X	X	0	0			X	0		0							0		0	X			0	0	C
	X	X	0	0			0												0				0	0	D
↘	↘	↗	↘	↗	↗	↗	↘	↘	↘	↗	↘	↘	↘	↗	↗	↗	↗	↗	↗	↗	↘	↗	↘	↗	

52	51	
X	0	A
X	0	B
X	0	C
X	0	D
↘	↘	

142

Pattern 74

Warp Ends: 216

Warp Breakdown: 120 = ☒
48 = ☐
48 = 0̄

9-31. Draft for Pattern 74.

25	24	23	22	21	20	19	18	17	16	15	14	13	12	11	10	9	8	7	6	5	4	3	2	1	
X	X	X	X	O	O	O			X	X	X	X	X	X	O	O	O				X	X	X		A
X		X	X	X	O	O			X	X	X	O		X	X	X	O	O			X	X	X	O	B
X			X	X	X	O		X	X	X	O	O		X	X	X	O		X	X	X	O	O		C
X				X	X	X	X	X	X	O	O	O			X	X	X	X	X	X	O	O	O		D
↗	↗	↗	↗	↗	↗	↗	↘	↘	↘	↘	↘	↘	↗	↗	↗	↗	↗	↗	↘	↘	↘	↘	↘	↘	

50	49	48	47	46	45	44	43	42	41	40	39	38	37	36	35	34	33	32	31	30	29	28	27	26	
		O	O	O	X	X	X	X	X	X				O	O	O	X	X	X	X	X	X	X	X	A
		O	O	X	X	X		O	X	X	X			O	O	X	X	X		X	X	X	X	X	B
X		O	X	X	X		O	O	X	X	X		O	X	X	X		X	X	X	X	X	C
X	X	X	X	X			O	O	O	X	X	X	X	X				X	X	X	X	X	D
↗	↗	↘	↘	↘	↘	↘	↘	↗	↗	↗	↗	↗	↘	↘	↘	↘	↘	↘	↘	↘	↘	↘	↗	↗	

54	53	52	51	
X	X	X		A
O	X	X	X	B
O	O	X	X	C
O	O	O	X	D
↗	↗	↗	↗	

Pattern 75
Warp Ends: 220
Warp Breakdown: 127 = X
                        42 = ■
                        28 = O
                        23 = ☐

9-32. Draft for Pattern 75.

25	24	23	22	21	20	19	18	17	16	15	14	13	12	11	10	9	8	7	6	5	4	3	2	1	
	X	X	X	■	■	O	O	O					X	X	X	X	X	X	X	X	X	X	X	X	A
O	X	X	X	X	X	■	■	■	O	O	O	■	■	■	X	X	X	X	X	X	X	X	X		B
■	X	X	X	X	X	X	X	X	■	■	■	O	O	O	■	■	■	X	X	X	X	X	X		C
X	X	X	X	X	X	X	X	X	X	X		O	O	O	■	■	■	■	■	X	X	X			D
╱	╱	╱	╱	╱	╱	╱	╱	╱	╱	╱	╱	╱	╱	╱	╱	╱	╱	╱	╱	╱	╱	╱	╱	╱	

50	49	48	47	46	45	44	43	42	41	40	39	38	37	36	35	34	33	32	31	30	29	28	27	26	
X	X	X	X	X	X	X			O	O	O	■	■	■		X	X	X		O		X		O	A
X	X	X	X	■	■	■	O	O	O	■	■	■	X	X	X	X	X	X	O		X		X	■	B
X	■	■	■	■	O	O	O	■	■	X	X	X	X	X	X	X	X	X	■	X			X		C
	O	O	O			X	X	X	X	X	X	X	X	X	X	X	X	X							D
╲	╲	╲	╲	╲	╲	╲	╲	╲	╲	╲	╲	╲	╲	╲	╲	╲	╲	╲	╲	╲	╲	╱	╱	╱	

55	54	53	52	51	
X	X	X	X	X	A
X	X	X	X	X	B
X	X	X	X	X	C
X	X	X	■		D
╱	╱	╱	╱	╱	

Bibliography

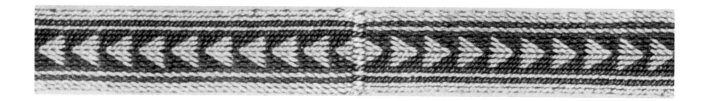

Atwater, Mary M. *Byways in Handweaving*. New York: Macmillan, 1954.

———. Mary M. "Card Weaving." Lily Mills Company, Shelby, North Caronlina.

———. "Notes on Cardweaving." New York: Universal School of Handicrafts, 1944.

———. "Stunting on the Cards." *The Weaver* 2 (1937): 25–30.

Black, Mary E. *Handweaver's Reference*. Bedford, Nova Scotia, 1954.

Bolland, Rita. "Three Looms for Tablet Weaving." *Tropical Man*, (Yearbook of the Department of Social Research, vol. 3), Amsterdam: Royal Tropical Institute, 1970.

Chapman, Ann. "Weaving Without a Loom." *Creative Crafts Magazine*, reprint from Lily Mills, Shelby, North Carolina.

Clifford, Lois I. *Card Weaving*. Peoria: Manual Arts Press, 1947.

Cobb, Eloise. "Bookmarks and Hair Bands on Card Weaving." *The Weaver* 7 (1942): 23.

Crowfoot, Elisabeth. "Braid Weaving Techniques in Ancient Egypt." *Liverpool Bulletin* 10 (1961–2): 22.

Crowfoot, Grace M. "A Tablet Woven Band." *Ancient Egypt*, December (1924): 98. London: British School of Archaeology in Egypt.

———, and Roth, H. Ling. "Were the Ancient Egyptians Conversant with Tablet Weaving." *Annals of Archaeology and Anthropology*, vol. 10. University of Liverpool, Institute of Archaeology, 1923.

Geijer, Agnes. *Oriental Textiles in Sweden*. Copenhagen: Rosenkilde and Bagger, 1951.

Goff, Russell E. *Card Weaving or Tablet Weaving*. McMinnville, Oregon: Robin & Russ Handweavers, 1969.

Hald, Margrethe. "Brikvaevning I Danske Oldtidsfund." *Aarbøger for Nordisk Oldkyndighed Og Historie*. Copenhagen: 1930.

———. *Brikvaevning*. Copenhagen: Gyldendalske Boghandel-Nordisk Forlag, 1932.

———, and Broholm, Hans C. *Costumes of the Bronze Age in Denmark*. Copenhagen: NYT Nordisk Forlag-Arnold Busck, 1940.

Henderson, Ethel, and Sandin, Mary. "Card Weaving." *Loom Music* 8 (1951): 51.

Hooper, Luther. *Tablet Weaving*. Weaving with Small Appliances. book 2. London: Sir. I. Pittman & Sons, 1923.

Jaques, Renate. *Encyclopedia of Textiles*. New York: Praeger, 1958.

Klein, A. "Tablet Weaving by the Jews of Sana' (Yemen)." Presented at the IXth International Congress of Anthropological and Ethnological Sciences, Chicago, 1973.

Lee, Thorold D. "The Linen Girdle of Rameses III." *Annals of Archaeology and Anthropology*, vol. 5. University of Liverpool, Institute of Archaeology, 1912.

Lehmann-Haupt, C. F. "Notes on the Linen Girdle of Rameses III," *Annals of Archaeology and Anthropology*, vol. 7. University of Liverpool, Institute of Archaeology, 1914.

McNulty, W. F. "Drawing Down Card Weaving Drafts." *The Weaver*, 6 (1941): 31.

Peach, Mabel. "Tablet Weaving." Leicester: Dryad Handicrafts, 1926.

Pope, Arthur Upham, with Ackerman, Phyllis. *A Survey of Persian Art from Prehistoric Times to the Present*, vol. 3. London: Oxford University Press, 1939.

Pralle, Heinrich. *Tablet Weaving—An Old Peasant Craft*. Leicester: Dryad Handicraft, 1920.

Schuette, Marie. "Tablet Weaving" *CIBA Review*, vol. 10. Basle, Switzerland: Society of Chemical Industry in Basle, 1956.

Staudigel, Otfried. "Tablet Weaving in Ancient Egypt." *Liverpool Bulletin*, vol. 9. Liverpool, 1960–1.

Stein, Sir (Mark) Aurel. *Serindia: A Detailed Report of Explorations in Central Asia and Westernmost China*. Oxford: Clarendon Press, 1921.

"Tablet Weaving," Dryad Leaflet 111. Leicester: The Dryad Press.

Thorpe, Heather G. "It's in the Cards." *Handweaver & Craftsman*, 3 (1952): 17.

Trotzig, Liv, and Axelsson, Astrid. *Weaving Bands*. New York: Van Nostrand Reinhold Co., 1972.

Van Gennep, A., and Jéquier, G. *Le Tissage aux Cartons et son Utilisation Décorative dans l'Egypte Ancienne*, Neuchâtel: Delachaux & Niestlé, 1916.

Youse, Clara M. "Card Weaving Technique." *The Weaver* 6 (1941): 26–30.

List of Suppliers

The following list is but a small sampling of the innumerable yarn shops throughout the country. Any trade magazine for weavers/spinners, etc., is rife with advertisements from the United States and around the world. The interested beginner would do well to start collecting samples from many different places to learn what types of yarns are on the market and how much they cost. Sample cards range in price from $.25 to $1.00; very few are free any more, as it takes a great deal of time and effort to put up samples. Remember, also, that a yarn offered today at one price may no longer be available from the same dye lot in six months and next year it may very well be more expensive.

Bartlettyarns, Inc.
Harmony, Maine 04942
Yarns (wools)

Berga/Ullman
Box 831
Ossining, New York 10562
Yarns (enormous selection of imported wools)

Bev's Yarn Shop
11 West 17th Street
New York, New York 10011
Yarns/Cards (wide range of wools; always a supply of oddments—the most unusual is the braided coconut fiber)

Clasgens Yarn Shop
Outlet #2
10861 Sharondale Road
Cincinnati, Ohio 45241
Yarns (mostly wools)

Contessa Yarns
Box 37
Lebanon, Connecticut 06249
Yarns (mail order only; always interesting offerings but availability changes)

Coulter Studios
118 East 59th Street
New York, New York 10022
Yarns/Cards (diversified inventory; fine quality wools, linens, cottons, etc. and an exquisite, natural-dyed silk)

Craft Yarns of Rhode Island
603 Mineral Springs Avenue
Pawtucket, Rhode Island 02862
Yarns (large variety of wools—all weights and colors)

Creative Fibers Studio
656 Millersport Highway
Buffalo, New York 14226
Yarns/Cards (wools as well as stunning combinations of synthetics)

Earth Guild
149 Putnam Avenue
Cambridge, Massachusetts 02139
Yarns/Cards (first-rate, extensive stock; everything from DMC embroidery floss to Finnish linens, to CUM wools)

The Fiber Studio
Box 356
Sudbury, Massachusetts 01776
Yarns (wools, novelties, synthetics; one of the few places for neutria)

Folklorico
Box 625
Palo Alto, California 94302
Yarns (many different kinds, including an elegant rayon floss and Icelandic wools)

Fort Crailo Yarns Company
2 Green Street
Rensselaer, New York 12144
Yarns (colorful line of wools)

Frederick Fawcett, Inc.
129 South Street
Boston, Massachusetts 02111
Linens (superior quality—all colors
and weights; some other items)

Greentree Ranch Wools
163 North Carter Lake Road
Loveland, Colorado 80537
Yarns (all types of wools, novelty yarns,
silks, goat's hair, etc.)

The Handweavers Studio and Gallery
29 Haroldstone Road
London, England
Cards (two different sizes with four holes
and one size with six holes)

Harrisville Designs
Harrisville, New Hampshire 03450
Yarns (lovely wools; also, top-quality
camel's hair, alpaca, and cashmere)

P. C. Herwig Company
Milaca, Minnesota 56353
Cards and various fibers

Lily Mills
Shelby, North Carolina 28150
Yarns/Cards (endless inventory—
wools, cottons, jutes, novelties, rayons,
linens—everything under the sun!)

The Loomery
3239 Eastlake Avenue East
Seattle, Washington 98102
Yarns/Cards (jute available in beautiful
colors)

The Mannings Creative Crafts
R.D. #2
East Berlin, Pennsylvania 17316
Yarns/Cards (varied stock items include
not only wools, but also feathers and
furs)

Naturalcraft
2199 Bancroft Way
Berkeley, California 94704
Yarns/Cards (all kinds of fiber—rattail,
jute, imported wools; cards are available
with three, four, and six holes)

Oldebrooke Spinnery
Mountain Road
Lebanon, New Jersey 08833
Yarns (handsome, diverse wools, many
naturally-dyed)

Paternayan Brothers
312 East 95th Street
New York, New York 10028
Yarns (handsome wools—several
weights and a garden of colors)

The Pendleton Shop
Box 233
Sedona, Arizona 86336
Yarns (many types of fiber—synthetics,
wools, jutes, etc.)

Robin and Russ Handweavers
533 North Adams Street
McMinnville, Oregon 97128
Yarns/Cards (a wide range of fiber stock
that is constantly changing)

Roycroft Handweavers
28 South Grove Street East
Aurora, New York 14052
Yarns (many unique items; some
polyester blends)

School Products
1201 Broadway
New York, New York 10001
Yarns/Cards (vast stock; vibrant cottons,
CUM wools, jutes, etc.; cards available
with three, four, and six holes)

Sheep's Kin
12 South 15th Street
San Jose, California 95112
Yarns/Cards (beautiful rya wool)

Some Place Handweavers
2990 Adeline Street
Berkeley, California 94703
Yarns/Cards (also available is a frame
for card weaving)

Tahki Imports
336 West End Avenue
New York, New York 10023
Yarns (the Irish imports are
exceptional)

Textile Crafts
Box 3216
Los Angeles, California 90028
Yarns (very large selection of popular,
known brands)

The Weaver's Store
273 Auburn Street
Auburndale, Massachusetts 02166
Yarns (well stocked with wide variety
of outstanding wools and other fibers)

The Weaving Shop
1708 Walnut Street
Boulder, Colorado 80302
Yarns (some interesting imports)

Clinton Wilkinson
6429 Virginia Avenue
Charlotte, North Carolina 28214
Yarns (stock constantly changing)

Yarn Depot
545 Sutter Street
San Francisco, California 94102
Yarns/Cards (infinite selection of
wools, linens, cottons, etc.)

Yarn Primitives
Box 1013
Weston, Connecticut 06880
Yarns (spectacular naturals, no
synthetics)

Index